ALIEN

Occam's

Razor

Series

Book One

∞∞∞∞∞∞∞∞∞

JD Lovil

COPYRIGHT

ALIEN

Occam's Razor Book One

Copyright © 2018 JD Lovil

ALL RIGHTS RESERVED

You may contact the author at the email address below:

jdlovilpublishing@gmail.com

ISBN: 978-0-359-40466-7

Independently published

DISCLAIMER

This is a work of nonfiction speculation. The subject matter of this book is open to extreme interpretations and viewpoints. The Author has taken the opportunity to add his discordant voice into the mix, with the hope of adding clarity to these muddy waters. If he cannot do that, he will settle for adding mud into these clear waters. Whatever works.

CONTENTS

ACKNOWLEDGMENTS

This book is based loosely on the concepts of many authors dealing with the subject of extraterrestrial life. I blame my youth wasted reading science fiction for my creation of this book.

A large part of the details for this book come from persons such as Zecharia Sitchin, Richard M. Dolan, J. Allen Hynek, and of course, Erich Von Daniken.

The publications of Lloyd Pye were also especially useful for information about all the reasons why our bodies show the hand of a genetic tinkerer, which has been busy designing us.

INTRODUCTION

O ccam's razor is a philosophical principle, applied to the field of scientific inquiry and to the resolution of logical arguments, which states that the simplest theory that explains all of the facts relating to the argument is probably the correct one.

Ask anyone about the possibility of alien life, and if aliens are visiting our fair planet, and you will probably get an answer that is unique for every person asked. Some people think that none of it is real, and an audience of billions of gullible people espouses belief in a delusion of alien visitation. Some people think that it is all real, and a vast conspiracy is in place to convince us that it is all a lie.

We live in a vast world, filled with human beings with opinions on this and a trillion other subjects. People hold contradictory theories about this subject, and they generally insist that their theory is the only true interpretation of the subject of aliens and alien visitation. Everyone else is obviously wrong.

They cannot all be right. There has to be a method to define the argument in such a way that it is possible to find the true answers in this ocean of wishful speculation that currently holds sway as the answers. It is time for a closer look at how to use the tool we call Occam's razor to find the answers.

Occam's razor is a principle that is more appropriate for scientific inquiry than it is for the normal argumentative procedure. Let me explain what I mean by that.

A scientific investigation has many of the elements of a logical argument. It assembles all of the known facts. It assembles the possible conditions and mechanisms that explain the facts. These are all speculated upon, and the hypotheses that are formed to explain the phenomena are advanced as tentative assumptions that are easily changed, eliminated, or abandoned. It eventually reaches a conclusion which explains the whole process under the investigation in every case.

The conclusion is the theory that we make out of the argument. If we find even one case in which the theory does not accurately explain the events, we must abandon that theory for an alternative explanation.

We find it to be quite useful to filter through our possible answers in such a scientific inquiry using Occam's razor. It works well as a tool to uncover the truth when the seeker has not already made up their mind about what is going on, but it might also be used to damage a logical argument where the participants have already decided what conclusions they wish to reach in the argument.

In either the scientific or the simple logical arguments, some components are essential to use in the argument's structure. Let us discuss the structure familiarly and informally.

As is true for any journey, an argument starts with some sort of roadmap. The two sides have to agree on the subject of the argument. In some forms of argument, they may also state their intended conclusions. In other forms, they will let the argument lead them to the conclusion.

They will assemble a set of assumptions that support their arguments. These will divide into two sets of assumptions. The first set will be the assumptions that both sides of the argument can agree are valid without revision. The second set will be the assumptions that are in dispute by one or both sides without revision, but that both sides may be persuaded to accept during the process of the argument.

The argument will need to supply facts and evidence to support any aspect of the argument that is not wholly accepted by the other side. In the case of the question of alien life and visitation, this might include testimonies of witnesses, photographic, and physical evidence, and various sorts of numerical analysis.

Rules will also be required to reach valid conclusions by logical means. One of the worst qualities of any form of argument is the tendency of one of the participants to 'drown out' their opponent, or overpower and intimidate them, to win by default.

Tune in any current political debate, and you will see one

side continue to talk out of turn and above the opponent's comments, to silence them. If I were the drowned out participant, then I would have one of two reactions.

I might tend to be somewhat sad that my opponent had so little logical thought that intimidation techniques were the 'go to' methods for their arguments, and wonder why the moderator had not switched off my opponent's microphone when they began doing the 'talk over.' I might also have the urge to reach over and rearrange their faces with extreme prejudice if I had an even slightly bad day.

This process of drowning out one side of the match is damaging in that it nullifies the purpose of the logical argument, and it allows the logical conclusion to be a flawed conclusion since it is based on competition rather than logic. Logic is a deliberative process, not a competitive process.

Because logic is deliberative, the persons who are good at using it are usually also deliberative and analytical, only presenting their points as factual points after careful scrutiny. This makes the logical personality slow to speak, and easy to be 'yelled down' by a more competitive person.

This all leads to a principle I like to call **the ten-year-old girl principle**. A two-hundred-pound man usually has nothing to fear from a match-up with a sixty-five or seventy-pound ten-year-old girl. All he has to do is retaliate with minimal strength, or subdue her by sitting on her or putting her in an arm or headlock. He can even just walk away.

If the man were to be restrained by rules that forced him

not to walk away, and not to attack or defend his self overtly or covertly, then he would suddenly find himself in danger. It might take a while, but the ten-year-old would eventually be able to beat the man to death.

When a person is engaged in an argument in a deliberative methodology, while his opponent is acting competitively, the competitive methodology will win, even though it does not achieve the results that they should be seeking. For any sort of valid investigative conclusion to be reached, both sides of the argument should be using the deliberative methods. When deciding which of several possible conclusions might be the correct one, use of Occam's razor is very useful.

Arguments are generally used as tools in two different ways. They may be used as a means to determine the truth in the subject they discuss, or they may be used to justify the conclusion that one or both of the participants wish to reach. I will give you two guesses about which way is the right way to use logic.

Logic is a way to lead the opponent to a conclusion about a subject, which is acceptable to both parties. This can be about actions to take, or this can be a process to understand. The conclusion can be a pre-determined conclusion that the first party wishes to convince the second party is the superior conclusion, or it can be a conclusion that is wholly determined by where the stairway of the acceptable assumptions leads.

While the steps of a logical argument must be logical, the conclusion may be irrational. For instance, consider the following idea:

I want a vehicle to drive to destinations in my life. It will be mostly in town on city streets, and I do not need a work truck, so a car will be acceptable. Four wheels, engine, and the normal accouterments are all necessary components.

I can let my logical ladder of assumptions and facts lead me to an arbitrary conclusion, and wind up with a Ford Fuckus, or some similar vehicle. Alternatively, I can start out with my secret desire for a red Corvette, and design my logical argument to reach the conclusion that the car is my perfect car. It all depends on what the purpose of the argument is as to which form my argument should take.

If I truly want to wind up with the perfect car for my needs, I probably will not be getting the red Corvette. If I need a proper ego stroking, then the Corvette is the only conclusion that will do.

If we call the two techniques of logical argument the investigative and the egocentric, then obviously the investigative is most useful for learning new things, and taking care to find the truth rather than your preferred lies. The egocentric is good for getting what you want, not for learning the truth. Both forms are used extensively in the subjects of alien life and visitations.

Once all of the assumptions and facts have been considered in the subject of all things alien, Occam's razor becomes absolutely necessary for determining which of the possible conclusions are the most likely ones to be the valid conclusions. In case you don't know how it goes, I will restate it below.

Occam's Razor- a philosophical principle, applied to the field of scientific inquiry and to the resolution of logical arguments, which states that the simplest theory that explains all of the facts relating to the argument is probably the correct one.

Some possible conclusions can be reached regarding the questions that we can raise about alien life. Here are some below.

1. Does alien life exist?

A Yes it does.

B No it does not.

2. Are aliens visiting earth?

A. No.

B. Yes.

3. Are the reports of alien visitors real events, delusions, lies, or mistaken reporting?

A. They are real.

B. They are not real but caused by lies, crazy people and mistaking Venus for flying saucers.

The number of possible questions to answer in this area is endless, and then there are the sub-questions to answer. For instance, if aliens are real, and visiting, are they good guys or are they bad guys? Do they *serve man*, or do they *serve man*, if you know what I mean?

We will be touching on the subjects that are the most common features of the ufology arena in the next few chapters. Things like illusions and psychological considerations, conspiracies by humans, aliens, or both, if they do exist, what do they want and do we want them to have whatever it is, and many variations of these considerations.

Buckle your seatbelts, and crank up your ion engines. It is time to go meet the aliens.

1 DRAKE'S EQUATION

The first aspect of the alien existence and visitation issue to consider is a matter of arithmetic. The xenophile that explores the reasonableness of alien life existing somewhere has a strong friend in the probabilities of existence of the aliens that the math can provide.

There are those people 'out there' who believe that our existence is unique in the universe, a state that has never been duplicated elsewhere. This is a question of belief, and that is not really subject to logic, but we can at least influence the least hard-core of the population to consider other possibilities.

As someone once said, there are facts, and then there are damn facts. The one true fact about the possibility of alien life is that we do not have sufficient information to make a valid guess, but we can speculate.

The only examples we have of the appearance of life in the universe is the example of earthly life on our own planet. We know from some of the extremophile life forms that life is capable of being tenacious once it arises, no matter how hostile the environment.

In 1961, a man named Frank Drake attempted to open a scientific discussion about the likelihood of alien civilizations capable of sending us a signal by radio or other methods to alert us to their existence. He constructed an equation now known as Drake's Equation to estimate the probability of these civilizations existing in the locations and timeframes necessary to contact us during the timeframe during which we would be able to receive the signals.

Frank, and the other members of the group, which had whimsically named themselves 'The Order of the Dolphin,' proceeded to come up with the equation, which was, and is, currently unsolvable. It was an equation which could calculate the number of intelligent civilizations currently in the galaxy. You use a number for how many habitable planets are in the galaxy, and how often intelligent life evolves on planets with life, and how long any such intelligent life will broadcast using the electromagnetic spectrum, before falling silent due to extinction or a technology shift. Currently, all of these numbers are, at best, educated guesses.

Drake came up with his equation, which calculates the number of broadcasting civilizations (N) in terms of seven variable terms, none of which are definitively known at this time. Let us go through the equation term by term, but first, let me complain about the problem that Frank attempted to solve.

I can imagine a host of ways in which a civilization might be high technology and available for contact by humanity without broadcasting on radio or radio analog wavelengths for all the universe to eavesdrop on. His number N should be the number of intelligent high technology alien civilizations currently operating in our galaxy.

The rest of the equation solves for either my or Frank's orientation on the problem equally accurately, substituting technological functioning civilization for broadcasting civilization. The equation is

$$N = R * f_p * n_e * f_1 * f_i * f_e * L$$

where:

N = # broadcasting civilizations or functioning technological civilization

R = Average rate of suitable star formations per year in our galaxy.

With an estimated star population of at least 100 billion, the formation of stars like our own in the galaxy is probably about one per year. Please note that it has recently been theorized that life could arise in a majority of the dwarf stars as well as yellow G stars. NASA puts star formation of all classes at about seven per year, of which I believe half might be good to support life-bearing planets.

f_p = Planet-forming stars as a fraction.

Our current exo-planet detections depend on occultisms and detection of gravity wobbles in star positions. Using these methods, we have found that 17% of the stars examined have close-orbiting planets, and 70% of stars examined have superjovian planets that can be detected by wobble and by examining light fluctuations as the planet passes in front of the star. The best guess is that there should be planets around at least 80% of the galaxy's stars.

n_e = habitable planets per star.

We have no certainty of any part of this variable at this time. The best we can do is assume that similar star systems with a similar number of distributed planets to our own solar system may also feature a similar number of habitable planets to our own. That would be one ideally habitable, one hostile habitable planet (Mars), and a number of icy moons such as Europa, where extremophile life forms might well flourish. There should be planets capable of supporting life on about 33% of the examined stars.

f_l = Fraction of planets (n_e) where life emerged.

This is another term we do not have the data for, but our own planet apparently developed life almost as soon as the surface solidified. Recent discoveries place the oldest fossils at 4.3 billion years old. The earth is only 4.54 billion years old. I suspect that most star systems will have at least one planet with life evolving there at some point. Call the fraction 0.9.

f_i = Fraction of life-bearing planets with life where intelligence evolved.

We have only ourselves as examples, so whatever number we pick would be a pure guess. Drake thought that 0.01 would be a good number. That would be one out of 100 life-bearing planets would develop intelligent life. I am still hoping it develops on earth. I think that every planet with life would eventually develop intelligent life if they have long enough. Call this fraction 0.5.

f_c = Fraction of planets with intelligent life that develops a means of interstellar communication that we can receive.

The problem here is that we do not know what alien means. If the aliens are all tool using primates, they will likely develop radio at some point. What if they are dolphin-like, or some other format of life that develops optic fiber or closed lasing systems, or even discovers how to use the process of quantum entanglement to create instantaneous communication? Drake put this one at 0.01. I would say that it is higher if we search meticulously, and we consider all imaginable means of communication. I would put this fraction closer to 0.1.

L = the average number of years an alien civilization will be detectable.

Since we are the only species that we know of with a

track record in this department, this is pure speculation. If other alien species are like our own, and we only assume that our period of delectability lasts until today, then we can probably assume that we became detectable a few years after Marconi's 1895 invention of the radio. Lob off a few years to increase signal strength to something that could transmit to other worlds, and say the average for human-like species might be 100 years.

To avoid depression, let us assume that most intelligent alien species will be relatively sane, so they will not ordinarily destroy themselves, or play in traffic with blindfolds on their heads. Some would probably last millions of years before something made them lose their technology or made them extinct. I think that a conservative estimate of the average years of high tech per alien civilization is at least 10,000 years.

You can see the numbers as I would plug them in below to come up with an estimate of higher tech civilizations in our galaxy. It does not account for things such as intentionally hiding or for species so alien that they would not produce any detectable indication of their existence.

$$N = R * f_p * n_e * f_1 * f_i * f_e * L$$

$$R = 3.5$$
$$f_p = 0.8$$
$$n_e = 0.33$$
$$f_1 = 0.9$$

$$f_i = 0.5$$
$$f_e = 0.1$$
$$L = 10000$$

I must be an optimist since my run of this equation with these guesstimates says that the number of high tech civilizations in this galaxy right now should be

$$N = 415.8$$

The Drake equation is pure speculation because we do not have verified numbers to plug into any of the variable values. As time goes on, we find more and more evidence that life arises everywhere that it is possible, and we have no reason to believe intelligence will not develop everywhere that life exists *eventually*. If you doubt that it is a common trait to develop, just watch an octopus solving problems sometimes. They are almost scary smart.

In the next chapter, we will start examining the volume of sightings of possibly alien events reported. We will then whip out our trusty Occam's razor to start trimming the lies from the truth.

2 TESTIMONY

It has been said that about one-fourth of the population of the planet has had a sighting of an unidentified flying object or even an encounter with entities, which fit our definitions of aliens. Nobody doubts that a good portion of these sightings and encounters are possible misinterpretations of less exotic events. There is a significant percentage of these sightings that cannot be easily explained away.

I was a resident of Phoenix, Arizona in 1997 when thousands of people observed the Phoenix lights. The condominium I was staying in had a patio that faced Camelback Mountain, over which the object was reported to travel.

I spent a lot of my free time on that patio, and I am chagrined to admit that I totally missed a sighting of the Phoenix Lights. Once again, I missed the good stuff.

I pride myself on being both skeptical and open-minded, and I would have loved to observe that event. Maybe I would have believed it to be an alien spacecraft, and maybe not, but fate took that opportunity away from me.

I consider myself a critical observer. I do not think that I will project my wishes and beliefs into a sighting. If it is clearly a vehicle of some sort, I believe that I will decide that is the truth, and if it looks like some strange alteration of the visage of Venus, I like to think that I will not try to see it as an alien vehicle.

In the millions of reports of unidentified flying objects both present and historical, there have been thousands of witnesses that we would ordinarily call unimpeachable. There have been Judges, Policemen, and all manner of professional observers and scientists of every type who have reported a close encounter or an aerial event.

Unless we are willing to suggest that we cannot trust our senses to deliver objective data to our brains, we must assign some level of validity to the testimony of these observers. We cannot trust that we know why the aliens are here, or what the aliens want, but trusting that something real is behind the events is necessary to our sanity.

While it is possible to postulate that there is no exterior objective reality, reaching such a conclusion has no possible positive consequences for us, only negative ones. In other words, we must believe in the existence of an objective reality, because without its existence, our existence and our belief structures have no validity, and may as well not exist, if they do indeed exist.

Our belief in the objective reality is the philosophical equivalent to a belief in a god or spiritual power that invests us with a destiny and a purpose. If we are wrong, it does not matter, since nothing else matters, but we get to spend some portion of our experience believing in a comforting deity. If we are right, then we get whatever treasures are traditionally dispensed to the believers. Can you say 'Win-Win'?

Persons have reported interactions with what we would call aliens for thousands of years, and across the world. Cultures with no contact with each other have reported amazingly similar contacts to each other. Isolated tribes in South America have reported contacts with creatures matching the standard 'Grey' alien descriptions, without ever hearing the stories of alien contact.

Before technology started allowing humans to see these events as alien, various land spirits, such as elves, sprites, and other elemental creatures were blamed for thousands of abductions, time loss, and other phenomena that now are all blamed on aliens. I have no doubt that the same tricks that the Pixies played on man are the alien tricks of the past.

The first written language that we are aware of is Sumerian, although a form of proto-Sumerian can be traced back to as much as thirty thousand years ago. I do not know about the backlog of stories from the Proto-Sumerian Arrata Empire writings, but in Sumerian writings proper there are obvious stories about visitors from the stars who interacted with humans on Earth.

Signs of celestial or alien actions have been recorded as occurring in the skies above many of the great battles of legend. Columbus recorded the antics of lights in the sky for much of his voyage to the new world. Virtually all of the

Founding Fathers of the United States believed that alien beings existed, and interacted with man.

We can get into the various sorts of physical evidence for the existence and visitation of aliens on Earth in later chapters, but for now, let us stick strictly to reported witnesses of alien activity. The sheer number of people who have reported activities that they believed to be alien activity is far too high to be a coincidence or any sort of common mental aberrations.

We can never discount the possibility that what we observe is not real. Since we live in a reality where certain rules seem to apply, let us examine the possibilities. We may possibly live in objective consensus reality, exactly as we see it daily.

We may live in a subjective but consensus virtual reality, or some illusionary equivalent to virtual reality. In this format, reality is an illusion, such as the virtual reality that you might immerse yourself in when playing an advanced computer game, but there exist multiple persons connected into that reality, and observing the same sets of events and laws as though the reality existed on a material matrix.

We may also live in a subjective virtual reality, where each of us is actually isolated in our own virtual world, where there is only one 'real person' in the world, but the rest of the world contains a virtual population. That world can also appear to conform to a consensus reality, although no 'real' consensus actually exists.

The world of thought is not black and white. I may have mentioned that not all logical arguments have to conclude with a rational conclusion. We construct our worlds of thought for our own benefit. Some conclusions that we could reach cannot benefit us to reach, and so we avoid reaching them. Consider the following scenario.

A group of you have been caught by the enemy. It is absolutely and conclusively known that the enemy will torture and eventually kill 100% of their captives over a period of time. Nobody has ever been captured and then escaped from them.

You have two choices. You can attempt to escape and have a chance to live. You can also just sit down and give up, just waiting to die. Which do you do?

Obviously, the only choice you can make that may benefit you is to attempt to escape. No matter what the chances are for your survival, it is still a higher chance than the zero chance of giving up and waiting to die.

The average person in this situation will actually sit down and show the pathetic face of depression because human instincts create the depressed state to influence the humans that surround us to help us out of a tight spot. In the interactions of an 'us or them' society such as a concentration camp, it usually works against survival, but most people will find themselves trying it anyway.

It is time to drag out Occam's razor. We can discount the individual virtual reality idea because it cannot be tested with dependably 'real' tools, and the validity of every rule, law, and event that such a reality can generate could never be validated regarding reality or value.

We can keep the concept of a consensus virtual reality,

which is large and intricate enough to be consistent with all rules, laws, and events that it contains. From within such a reality, there would be no way to determine whether it is real or virtual. Treating it as real should return the same answers, benefits, and timelines or worldlines as any objective reality.

We can make an assumption in regards to the question of objective or subjective realities. Either the reality that we function within is subjective and inconsistent, hence making it impractical to draw conclusions about any component events, or it is consistent in a subjective or objective mode, so valid conclusions can be drawn regarding the component events and laws.

This means that it may be that there are illusionary aspects to our experiences of what we perceive of as experiences of alien events. Once we have conducted due diligence in discerning such illusions, we should assume that that which appears to be real must be treated as real. In other words, if we see an unidentified flying object, we should check for mirages, illusions, and possible mental manipulations, and once we have screened those out of probability, we should accept the reality of whatever we observe.

If it looks like a flying saucer, and we have eliminated the subjective reasons for seeing it there in the sky, we should accept its reality, and move on to asking ourselves whose it is and why it is there. A little study of the forces that keep it flying would be fun, as well.

I do not know if he really ever said this, but Sigmund Freud famously said that sometimes a cigar is just a cigar.

He was hinting that once you had eliminated the likely sexual symbolism from the dream symbols, it might be that the cigar was exactly what it appeared to be, a cigar.

That was a crude example of using Occam's razor to say that the simplest solution is the real solution. Once you have sorted through the possible explanations, you should choose the simplest explanation that explains all of the facts. It is almost always the correct explanation.

Let us apply Occam's razor to the problem of alien visitations, and the existence of aliens. We have demonstrated in the previous chapter that the likelihood of alien life arising, and spawning intelligent life is very high. We do not have sufficient information to render a definitive probability, but with all available information, it would be unlikely that we are alone in the universe.

We have established that humanity has reported high numbers of events involving what appears to be alien visitors for centuries. We have also suggested in the first part of this chapter that we should assume that the events observed are real events, and not subjective and illusionary. The rest of this book will be devoted to establishing the cause of those events.

What are the questions that we want to answer? We want to know whether we are alone or we are not alone. We want to know if aliens are truly visiting us here on Earth. If they are, we want to know where they come from. We want to know what technology or art they use to get here. We want to know why they come here, and what their intentions are toward us. Are they competition, or friends?

These questions and a lot of variations of them are the questions we hope to begin to answer in the next few chapters. Get ready to question reality!

3 OBSERVATION

Everyone who has watched a few police drama television shows know that you interrogate the witnesses separately. In the shows, it is understood that you separate witnesses to keep them from knowing what lies to tell, but it is also useful for noncriminal witnesses.

Observation is an interpretive process. If a hundred people who stood in a crowd and watched an event were asked separately what happened, you would hear a hundred stories with subtle or even major differences in the event details.

Any evidence or assumption built on the observations of people is subject to this problem. A trained observer is trained to limit their emotional investment in a pet theory about what an event means. Let us explain that with the use of your standard cop as an example.

Most police officers that have been on the job more than a year or two tend to be a little pessimistic about the good intentions of anyone that has a significant record. If a potential culprit has a record, the officer is likely to unconsciously tilt their reporting of the actions of that person to a bias towards guilt. Meanwhile, the suspect's mother is equally certain that her little boy could have never done such a heinous thing, whatever it was.

We are all built that way. If we see twenty black guys in hoodies hanging out under the streetlight in a deserted section of road, we tend to profile them as potentially dangerous and find another way home.

Some of us may think that any aliens we might encounter are messengers of light. If so, it is likely that any actions we see them engaged in will support that notion. If we do not believe in aliens, it will take much more to convince us that the light in the sky is an alien craft than it would if we already thought they might exist.

Just like the actor pretending to be a cop in the show will separate witnesses to interview them, we will get the best results in evaluating witness reports by interviewing them separately, and then checking all of the reports to see what factors they have in common. When a housewife in Phoenix, and a bushman in Africa both report the same description of an alien, even though the bushman never saw a movie or television, there may be something real there.

Again, we are ignoring the possibility that we live in a consensus virtual reality, where all of this is in our heads, but there are many of us all dreaming the same dream with the same rules, so to speak. We cannot refute that idea, but if it is the case since that world acts just like the 'real' world, we can treat it as if it is true.

If this *is* the real world or one that acts real, then we can address the possible causes of any events we experience, one by one, and eventually, we will be able to eliminate all of the answers that are not consistent with the reality.

For instance, we know that mass and individual psychology, illusions, delusions, and psychic activity could be the causes of the events we think that we experience. If we can find consistent reporting of identical events in different environments with different numbers of observers and with observers with different temperaments and psychic sensitivities, we can eliminate most of the 'non-real' causes of the events.

There are certain aspects of modern contact reports that are too subjective to be considered as objective facts. Contactees frequently report what they believe is telepathic contact with the aliens, and many of them have an overwhelming sensation of the aliens as being absolutely beneficent. A few of the files report the aliens as being absolutely evil. These are all subjective interpretations by the witnesses that must be considered suspect.

Assuming that an alien contact is a real event, as third parties, we have no way of determining if the aliens are truly communicating telepathically, or if the witnesses are 'filling in the gaps' of the experience from any of possibly thousands of urges, beliefs, and psychological interactions. If the communication is real, then we still do not know if the message conveyed is the Truth or a Lie.

There are severe limitations on the validity that we can place on the testimonies of witnesses. I believe that we have adequately expressed why they always must remain suspect.

Lucky for us, there are forms of evidence that are less suspect that we can still examine. It is always a good day when we can get our hands on an artifact, or some physical evidence of possible alien activity, such as crop circles, radioactive spots, or a bit of technology or effects of that technology.

We can also explore the nooks and crannies of history, looking at megastructures, mythology, and archeology. We can also look at ourselves, since many of the old stories describe how we were created, or modified, by the old gods. The old gods were *obviously* alien visitors.

Observation will always be a fertile and useful field of study to determine what pieces of the alien inquiry is ripe for examination. It can never be the sole source of evidence for this subject, just as a body or a murder weapon is usually needed to clinch a murder case, even if the prosecution has plenty of witnesses.

4 FLIGHT TECHNOLOGY

Evidence for the existence and actions of aliens abound in the form of technology. This covers everything from technological artifacts recovered, historical reports of technology that indicates knowledge that requires that technology to be known for the humans of the time to possess the knowledge and required technology for the actions of the aliens that are reported to be accomplished. In this chapter, we will aim primarily at flight technologies.

In the next chapter, we will deal with non-flight related technology, such as the implants, along with various building techniques and ancient knowledge that requires a space-faring population to acquire. Either aliens or space-faring humans would be required to know certain things that ancient civilizations knew.

First, let us start with a few working assumptions. The entities we see as aliens could come from several possible places. They could be from Earth, hidden away from humanity. They could be from a parallel universe, using unknown means to come to our universe. They could live on one of the other planets or moons in our system, or they could actually come to Earth from one of the many stars in our galaxy.

The standard report of the possible alien vessels requires some exotic technology to accomplish the actions seen. The craft have been seen to hover motionless in the sky for extended periods, and then they can accelerate to extreme speeds in a very short period of time, at speeds that are multiple times the speed of sound, without emitting a sonic boom, or any other noise.

To accomplish the maneuvers that have been reported, the craft would have to have exquisite control over both gravity and of inertia. They must also have some technology that can defeat the buildup of air density along the edges of the craft that is responsible for the whiplash effect that produces the sonic boom as the craft velocity becomes greater than the speed of sound.

If we make the standard assumptions that the aliens are real, and come from another star, they may make the transit at speeds below the speed of light. If they are biologically or psychologically at all similar to humans, it is unlikely that they would make the trip if they had to invest so many years and effort into the visit, unless the purpose was to transfer large populations to Earth as a second home.

There is no indication that they are attempting to colonize Earth, at least not with their original population. There may be an attempt to hybridize the human species, but that would not help reduce their own populations, so I do not think that they plan to colonize.

This means that it is likely that they make the trip to Earth using some faster than light technology. This probably means warp or wormhole technology, along with some substantial shielding tech to prevent the vehicle from being vaporized when colliding with space dust.

Now that we have briefly mentioned the needed tech to get our visitors, and to explain what their craft can do, let us see if we can explain it in a little more detail. To start the voyage here, they must have developed a high degree of control over gravity expression in their vicinity and used it to develop a workable warp technology.

We will discount the wormhole technology for now. It would likely prove to be as hard or harder to create than warp tech, which would result naturally from gravity control research.

Einstein described gravity in simple geometric terms as deformation in spacetime due to the presence of mass. The higher the mass density in a region, the higher the deformation of spacetime and that deformation expressed itself as a gravetic attraction to the center of mass for nearby masses, like a marble rolling down a hill to the position of least energy, which in this case is to the mass at the bottom.

There are some indications that space can be deformed in this way by many forces, such as intense electromagnetic fields, and of course movement of masses. Assuming that the aliens find suitable tools to deform spacetime appropriately, at some point they may be able to strongly curve spacetime or to smooth it as they desire.

This would have the effect of being able to change the effects of gravity on objects, making them 'lighter' or 'heavier' as desired. In other words, with a lot of tinkering, it might be possible to create a gravity control technology.

With gravity tech, you could create spacecraft that would hover weightless above planets, but that is just the start. Once you can manipulate gravity, warp technology is just a couple of steps away.

Einstein's Theory of Special Relativity said a number of important things. It spoke of events in terms of Frames, and it said that nothing could exceed the speed of light. That might sound like warp travel at multiple times the speed of light cannot happen, but it does not really say that. Let us talk about Frames.

Imagine that there are a space station and a bar on the station run by a man named Frank. He has a mean streak, a laser pistol, and two acquaintances named Joe and Sue that owe him money. Sue has jumped into her spaceship and is currently traveling at just under the speed of light, heading out toward Tau Ceti, and Joe is doing the same thing in the opposite direction, flying hell-bent for Wolf 359.

All three of them have a magical telescopic viewer so they can see each other from anywhere, and Frank's laser has the magical ability to make super bright laser beams that everyone can see. Frank is mad and very drunk, so he steps to the airlock and starts firing at Joe's ship.

Joe's and Sue's ships are moving away from each other at nearly twice the speed of light since they are each moving at nearly the speed of light in opposite directions. Frank's laser can only approach Joe's position at the speed of light, so it overtakes Joe only by the difference between the speed of light and Joe's speed.

Einstein said that the speed of light was the same everywhere. If you call the spaceships and the space station each a separate Frame, it is no surprise that Joe, Sue, and Frank each sees the laser overtaking Joe at the speed of light. This is so since the velocity of Joe's Frame that each one sees from their perspective is exactly compensated by the time dilation effects of their relativistic speeds.

It is an accepted fact that spacetime is expanding in the universe. Like an expanding balloon, points widely separated in space are increasingly separated by the expansion of spacetime. Some of the most distant regions of the universe appear to be expanding at more than the speed of light.

If Joe and Sue could make spacetime expand or contract around them, then they could cause the Frame that contains their spaceships to travel through the stars at speeds far above the speed of light, without ever making their spacecraft exceed the speed of light within their Frame. That is how you make a warp drive.

Once you create gravity drives, you can curve and smooth spacetime as desired. It is easy to curve space ahead of your ship, and smooth it behind your ship, making the distance to travel ahead of you much shorter than normal, and making the distance behind you much further than you had to travel.

Notice that you never have to exceed light speed using warp technology, since the major movements are in the flow of spacetime, not the movement of the mass of your ship. Indeed, your ship might even be able to travel at a sedate non-relativistic speed, reducing the stresses and shielding needed to make the trip.

You will still want to have an actual velocity of several thousands of miles per hour, but traveling at ninety or more percent of light speed is likely to be unnecessary and unwise. Even the smaller speed would demand highly efficient shielding methods to protect the ship against micro and macro impacts, but nothing like what would be needed at relativistic speeds.

So far, we have discussed technology that can make interstellar travel feasible, but gravity control may not translate into a feasible ship's drive on its own. Just because your ship can float does not necessarily mean that it will do any significant travel.

I grant you that control of gravity should be at least as useful as a solar sail for providing motive power for the ship, but I doubt that you would want to use it as your primary ship's drive. You have a ship that bobs in the wind, and you can probably get it to move by generating high gravity regions in front of the ship, but it seems a little unwieldy, and probably not eco-friendly.

What you need is a way to control the inertia of your ship. The gravetic drives described in most science fiction ships are not really gravity controlling devices, they appear to control both the gravity and the inertia of the mass of the spacecrafts.

Unfortunately, inertia is a poorly understood force. It is the thing that makes the universe obey the rule that 'a body put into motion will maintain that motion until acted on by another outside force.'

The UFOs could not make those high-speed changes in motion without a fine control over the inertia of the vehicles. Gravity control would not do it. Let me describe what I mean.

If you stand here on Earth, you feel a one gravity force acting on your body from the mass of the Earth beneath your feet. If you are standing in a spaceship that can generate a 1 G gravity, you are in exactly the same situation as if you stood on Earth.

If the Earth you were standing on suddenly took a hard left turn and headed off into deep space with a sudden high acceleration, your body would attempt to continue in the direction it was originally going, and you would go flying off the Earth in the original direction.

If the same thing happened on the spacecraft, you would also go flying off in the original direction, but you would soon impact on a ship's bulkhead with tremendous speed. It is a quick way to go see Jesus, but it would be less than satisfactory as a way to travel.

If you devised the technology, you could create an inertial drive. Nobody knows how to go about controlling inertia, but it is a property of mass that is significantly linked to other mass-related properties, which includes gravity.

It is not too much of a stretch to assume that if you

developed gravity control, you would also be able to figure out how to manipulate inertia. With that ability in hand, you would be easily able to change the momentum of all parts and contents of your spaceship to change the direction and speed of travel sharply, without even feeling any of the bad effects of acceleration.

Once you control inertia, you will be able to sit and calmly drink your coffee while your ship makes a right turn at full speed, followed by a high-speed contorted flight. You should also be able to accelerate your spaceship at any rate and in any direction that you wish.

The inertial drive would deliver a near perfect propellant-free thrust. No more rocket ships needed. We would no longer need to stress about the G-forces because we would not experience them.

The final problem we have to suggest a fix for is the problem of traveling at speeds above Mach 1 without generating a sonic boom. The engineers of the old SST were unsuccessful in eliminating the boom.

They were operating under the old idea that if you could make the profile of thc plane cut through the air like a very sharp knife, the air would not build up in front of the airplane that would cause the boom as the speed of Mach 1 was reached.

I believe that they might have had the right idea, but it would have been necessary to extend the blade profile far enough to achieve an almost absolute zero profile for the craft. It would need to extend far enough to make the slight protrusions of the craft, such as the cockpit and the engines disappear into an extended blade-like surface.

If aliens have force field technology, they might be able to extend those fields sufficiently to achieve a low enough profile. If they have strong enough magnetic field generators, they could also use a magnetic field to induce a dipole charge in the air molecules ahead of them. Once the molecules were charged, they could be pulled out of the line of flight by the field. Hence they would not build up in front of the craft. That means that there would be no sonic boom.

It is time to start wrapping this chapter up, so let us relate everything we have discussed so far in terms of Occam's razor. In the beginning, we decided that we should treat reports of alien actions and events as reports of real events.

In this context, real is defined as made of actual physical matter and obeying science, not magic or psychology. We will treat any report that is not falsifiable as a report of an event involving real vehicles and entities.

We recognize that there are uncounted thousands of these reports that are filed yearly. Over the last few decades, millions of interesting reports have been filed, and history shows that people have been reporting the same sorts of reports for all of recorded human history.

Among the witnesses of possible alien events, many of the witnesses are what we would generally consider being unimpeachable sources. Many of these reports appear to have no non-alien explanations. At some point, it becomes more of a stretch to think that no aliens are visiting us than it does to believe that they are all around us.

We know that if they are aliens from other star systems, and if they are like us in any way, they must develop certain technologies before they could make the trip. Unless they want to spend hundreds of years making the trip to Earth, they have to develop a faster-than-light spacecraft. This would most likely be a warp-drive ship, and it would probably have gravity control, with a reaction-less drive as the ship's drive, possibly an inertial drive.

They would also almost certainly have to develop an extremely effective shielding technology. With these technologies in place, they would be ready to explore the neighboring stars.

5 EARTHLY ARTIFACTS

The world is full of artifacts that support the idea of aliens physically visiting the Earth, and leaving their tourist trash all over the place. Different conclusions can explain parts of the evidence, but actual visiting aliens are the only explanation that seems to explain most or all of the evidence.

There is strong but strange evidence of hominoid beings, which might be aliens, or indigenous hominoids, in the deep past, and various bits of evidence that come out of the historical and sometimes the prehistorical records. We will start with some of the current and recent past, and work our way back.

Some strange behaviors and events appear in reports of the assumed alien activities, in current times as well as historically. There are also striking parallels to the activities of mythical beings in folklore, such as fairies, elves, and such creatures.

The Sidhe of Celtic myth behaved suspiciously like

current tales of alien actions. When the gods of the Celts had to give way to Christianity, the minor deities of their folklore became magical creatures that hid within the bowers and shadows of the wild places.

The Sidhe were credited with creating the 'fairy rings,' which were the odd, perfectly circular growth of mushrooms caused by the biochemistry of each mushroom staking out its own territory. They were also credited with the crop circles that occasionally were found in the grain fields.

The Sidhe were famous for their tendency to abduct people. The folklore started to focus on the abduction of children primarily, but they also inspired many tales of abductions of adults in their time.

People who were unfortunate enough to run afoul of the Sidhe frequently found that they had 'lost time,' sometimes just minutes, but some lost days, weeks, or even years of their lives.

The fairy folk of most traditions had a reputation for being Tricksters. In this context, much of what they did was incomprehensible and annoying, but not necessarily evil or good. The result of interactions with fairies generally was damaging to the human's lives, but it seemed as though the sprites were unconcerned about any damage done, not actively seeking to harm their target human.

The reason why I brought the fairy folk, especially the Sidhe, up so early in this chapter, is because I have always been struck by the similarities between these old myths and the reported events involving alien contacts. In most cases, substituting an alien 'grey' into any of the old fairy tales as the fairy would not change the story at all.

Thousands of humans disappear on Earth, some of them never to be seen again, and some stumble back into society after varying lengths of time with strange tales or with no idea why they disappeared. Some of the ones that reappear turn up in places and circumstances that would require significant help to get them into and in conditions that are inconsistent with the time and circumstance of their disappearance.

There have been hundreds of millions of accumulated reports of reports of flying UFOs or encounters with aliens over the last few decades, all over the world. Some of these reports included memories of abduction.

A large number of disappearances are never connected to alien activity. Does anyone want to guess how many of the other disappearances are abductions that were never reported? Perhaps the victim did not remember, or did not want to be called a liar, or never was returned.

Another standard bit of alien evidence is the elusive implant. The anti-UFO group would like you to believe that nobody ever actually has seen one, but that is a lie. Some very strange organic and metallic objects have been removed from the bodies of Experiencers. I do not believe that anyone has managed to figure out how they work, but there has been no shortage of recovered implants.

It has been assumed that these small objects have been put into the victims during an abduction to keep track of the person, for future retrieval and study. These objects do have a tendency to go missing after a period of time in the hands of a human.

This might be a self-destruct process or simple theft by unknown thieves. Most of them have endured extensive testing in the lab before going missing. A few of them have not disappeared.

One of the more fascinating events under the umbrella of alien activity is crop circles. These are complicated shapes and glyphs impressed into crop fields or sometimes wild-grain fields, with enough reports of associated alien events to convince us that the aliens themselves are responsible for the artwork.

The crop circles usually depict geometric shapes, pictographs, and what seems to be some form of alphabetic script. The script shares elements of ancient and arcane runic forms. The crop circles can appear in a stand of plants within minutes, far quicker than any human agency could accomplish it by any reasonable means.

Some people have come forward to claim responsibility for making these crop circles, but the evidence says otherwise. There are a few easy ways to tell if humans have faked a crop circle.

For humans to fake a crop circle, typically, they tie a heavy board with a lead rope at both ends, and then they drag that board through the crop plants, pushing them to the ground as the board is dragged over them. This results in crushed plants, which are bruised and scraped as the board is dragged over them.

This results in a badly disfigured fake circle, with uneven

borders and lines, and many plants in distress. A crop circle created by non-human means does not have any of these defects, and it has some other exciting differences.

In theories covering electromagnetic forces, we discuss the ideas of conductivity and magnetic properties of the materials. These terms are relative.

If you raise the voltage enough, every so-called nonconductor becomes a conductor, and if you raise the strength of the magnetic field enough, all matter becomes responsive to the charges inherent in a magnetic field.

There are materials within all living things, including plants, which have differing susceptibilities to magnetic fields. Every cell contains forms of salts, called electrolytes, which are instrumental to carrying water and nutrients into the cells, and long string hydrocarbons including proteins, which have many hydrogen atoms that can be manipulated by magnets.

A strong magnetic field can align those electrolytes along the field. This brings us to the interesting situation that we sometimes find when the human creation of a crop circle has been ruled out.

Observers occasionally report one of the typical alien craft hovering above the site. Sometimes, it is not a definable flying saucer they saw, but a hovering ball of light or energy.

If they observe the craft or light appear to land close to the crop circle, they will sometimes see small, burned areas, in that same place when they approach to investigate afterward. It looks as though something with a hot exhaust or high energy landed or hovered above the spot.

In the case of some of the un-refuted crop circles, a measurement of the magnetic field in the area around the plants using a gauss meter shows that the electrolytes and the other chargeable bits of the plants have been aligned in the same pattern as a magnetic field that had been applied to them. The field had laid the plants down in the precise patterns that the field expressed, with no bruising or scraping of the plants.

There have also been some bizarre items discovered all over the world. Everyone has heard of the Bagdad battery, which was a crude battery that obviously held stored energy for some function. This was a useless sort of thing to have around unless you also had some electrical appliances that needed the energy. We are pretty sure the Egyptians did not have light bulbs. Maybe they kept a power supply on hand in case alien visitors came by and wanted to read after dark?

Other odd things have been found, although nobody can really decide whether they are alien or just some out of place human stuff. There have been human footprints found in fossilized mud from around thirty million years ago, and from a couple of hundred million years ago. Everyone has probably seen the screw that was discovered dating back several million years. Then, there is the Ketz ball.

These strange metallic balls have been found all over the world. Most of them have been treated like inexplicable metal balls and forgotten. It was not until the 1970's that someone thought to check one out a little more closely.

The Ketz family found a sphere after a wildfire. The strange metal ball seemed to have a mind of its own. It would follow people around, rolling sedately along behind them. It would stop and start without concern for if it was rolling uphill or downhill

The Ketz family called the friendly little ball the Ketz sphere since you had to call it something. First, they examined the thing, and then they called in a few of their more scientifically minded friends, who also had a go at the ball. After a while, the Navy got wind of the sphere's existence, and they ruined the party by hogging the thing all for themselves.

Examination indicated that three smaller spheres were located inside the sphere, and an element with at least an atomic number of 140 was inside. This is at least 48 elements in the chart further than any naturally occurring element of which humanity was aware.

We will be getting into the following subjects in much more depth in the following chapters, but let us briefly mention other oddities that can stand as evidence of alien activity. The first oddity is the choice of architecture.

During the long history of Man, I do not believe that there have ever been long stretches of time with such an overabundance of luxury that humanity could afford to overbuild their buildings. Let me explain what I mean.

When humans were all hunter-gatherers, and human populations were very low density, it was easy to get whatever food you needed for the day, if it existed, and spend all sorts of time just lazing about in the sun. Once we started growing crops, it actually took a lot more work to make sure that we could keep up the habit of eating every day.

Humans spent most of the time tending to the crops and herds in city life. It didn't make a lot of sense wasting some of that time building something that took extreme efforts when any roof provided shelter.

Throughout the world, there are hundreds and thousands of huge buildings and structures built with multi-ton stone that we could not move with our current technology. How the ancients moved those stones into position is still a mystery.

In the area of the world that is now the country of Pakistan is a region with some strange features. There is an extensive area of the sandy terrain that is covered with radioactive glass, the same sort of glass that grows where nuclear weapons have been used. We will discuss that soon, but for now, the physical evidence and some very old myths agree with each other.

The last source of tantalizing evidence that we will discuss here is ourselves. I do not know how much you realize how odd we are, but genetically, we fit the old saying 'rode hard and put away wet, and half-finished.'

Our closest relations in the animal kingdom is the primates, who have ten times our strength for their sizes, who have far fewer genetic diseases than we do, and who *fits* their world far better than we ever could.

We cannot produce vitamins C or E. We have 23 pairs of chromosomes instead of the 24 of our nearest relatives.

Our ankles are too far back on the foot for efficient locomotion, and our ankles are extremely vulnerable to 'springing' them. No, we are almost certainly a half-finished science project that nobody thought to turn off before they abandoned it.

We can go on and on about evidence of the existence of alien interactions with our planet. We can, but let us cut it short here. We can get more in-depth in future chapters.

6 RECURSIVE ANTHROPIC PRINCIPLE

We have stirred a few of the anthills of our discussion. We have introduced a few of the interesting tidbits of data that will go into our arguments about the nature of all things alien. It is time to introduce a new concept that will complement the Occam's razor filter of our mental wanderings.

The first thing we need to do is to recognize why we set up our logical arguments in the investigation of our subject of interest. Our whole purpose is to reach a preferred conclusion while holding out our reasoning for persons with other viewpoints to falsify, or grudgingly to admit to our reasoning's validity.

It is important for you to realize that why are building a framework of logic to reach our conclusion, which may or may not be the most rational conclusion to reach, but that is the one that we prefer among all of the possible conclusions that have not been falsified. Let us use an example to demonstrate that once more.

Assume that you are hungry, and you have to argue about what to eat before you can fill your belly. You have some potatoes, and you have some pears, but you can have only one of the two choices. The rest will be sent to the needy down the road, and everyone here has to eat the same thing.

You prefer the pears. Some of the other people think that the potatoes are the best thing to eat, but you love pears. Everyone sets up their assumptions for the argument. The assumptions that all persons agree are valid become the bases of the argument.

Now assume that the arguments are set up to answer the arbitrary question of 'what is the best food to eat?', and you are arguing about six different foods instead of the original two. One of the foods is spinach, and nobody in your group likes spinach, although everyone agrees that it is a very nutritious food.

Since nobody likes spinach, nobody chooses to argue for eating it when it comes time for them to argue for a food. Even though it might win a totally logical argument about which food is the best one to eat, it will not be chosen.

The standard Anthropic Principle states that the reason why the universe, or world, seems suspiciously suited to us is that we have evolved here. If it had been too inhospitable, we would not be here to render our opinion.

In the same sense, the Recursive Anthropic Principle is the idea that we should only actively seek conclusions that benefit us. If there are foods on the list that are comparatively suitable to the spinach to eat that none of us like, then why waste time to argue for something we do not want?

We would still want to gather data about the nutrition value of the spinach. If a couple of foods wind up being essentially tied for the winner, then someone might use the spinach data to beat the one they do not want, provided it does not defeat their own choice.

If the argument was between prisoners of war about the prospects of escape, then one of the most likely conclusions to reach is that escape is impossible. The RAP tells us that considering an argument in favor of that defeatist conclusion is counterproductive, and should not be done.

Once the arguments are completed, there might well be two or more winning conclusions, and you need a tiebreaker. That would be the time to apply Occam's razor, to see which of the choices would be the simplest and most complete solution to the problem. If the conclusions are equally valid, it would be time to apply the RAP once again, to decide which of the choices is the more desirable one.

The RAP is a filtering method that I try to apply to the decision process wherever I can. I call it the *Recursive* Anthropic Principle because the universe picks by its nature the environment that shapes us. Our nature then looks at that environment and pronounces it good. In decisions of varying desirability, if the mind created in the universe that seems to follow the Anthropic Principle then applies a decision process that promotes the highest desirable outcome of its choices, this is a kind of recursive process.

The RAP is a handy companion filter to Occam's razor.

In our world, it is necessary to believe that in large part, we can accept what we receive from seeing, hearing, and other senses the events that happen around us.

It is not provable that our senses are actually validating the existence of a real world around us unless we can find a way to check our information from a position outside the system that is beyond the influence of anything within the system. In other words, we can never be sure.

Occam's razor would tell us that a universe of illusion is too complicated to be the valid answer. It is not actually saying that it is not the truth, but it is saying that it complicates the conclusions to the degree that they become useless.

There is no way to invalidate the idea that the universe might be a holographic or data-driven construct. It may be holographic in nature, but so perfect a construct that we cannot know if it is real or not real. It may be as real as it seems to be, which would allow us all to hold on to our sanity for a few moments more.

The Recursive Anthropic Principle says that the illusionary universe is not desirable for any mind that desires to find meaning, consistency, or purpose in existence within that universe. The best universe would be one that has a physical reality that is consistent with the universe that we think we are observing.

The RAP also cannot refute the complete Holographic universe, but if we are to be honest with ourselves, there are certain aspects of that universe that we find so necessary to our mental health that we insist on believing that those aspects exist, as we need them to exist. For instance, in that perfect Holographic world, we see a population of our fellow humans living around us.

Is that world truly filled with human holographs with unique minds? Alternatively, is it merely scenery for our entertainment? For that matter, are we even real?

Even if the world is not made of real matter, humans are social creatures, and we need them to be more than imaginary friends. No matter how realistically they act, if the people we see around us are only the next act in an environmental sensory drama, then our loneliness cannot be quelled by their imaginary actions, any more than the characters on your television provides true companionship.

The Razor tells us that the illusionary universe was too complicated, but the Holographic or Real universes were both viable choices. RAP tells us that only the Real universe or versions of the Holographic universe that provide emotionally, socially, or intellectually validating aspects are acceptable.

In other words, the Holographic universe is only an acceptable choice if all of those people we see in it are as real as are we, whatever real means in that context. In short, only if the Holographic universe is so perfect that it can never be revealed as unreal under any circumstance is it okay. Hence, only a real universe is acceptable.

The observer has to admit that he can never be 100% sure that the universe is real. Since the observer cannot be sure, after checking the universe for evidence of unreality, we should assume that the world is real, and act as if it is real from the moment we make that assumption onwards, as long as no future data proves it wrong. Such a conclusion passes both Occam's razor and the Recursive Anthropic Principle.

From this point on, we will assume that the world we see is the real one. Subjective data such as events of perceived telepathic communication, or other subjective phenomena such as objectivity of reports can be suspect, but we should assume any hard evidence to be exactly what it presents itself to be, which is hard evidence.

The next chapter will be devoted to catching us up on the history of events and stories that are suggestive of alien involvement in the human world. After that, we will begin to have some real fun!

7 HISTORY AND PREHISTORY

The most lenient of evolutionists say that the first primates appeared on planet Earth about 35 million years ago. They were probably less obviously primates than are the Lemurs of today, but that is what our learned scientists decided, so it must be so.

It is assumed by the modern evolutionary theory that modern man has been the result of several million years of progressive mutations from the primate genetic line. The fact that the linage is not in agreement with any smooth progression that has ever been postulated has strangely never been noticed.

As a matter of fact, the whole of human history seems to be a matter of sudden appearances. For instance, the most recent genetic information reveals that the Neanderthal is actually a parallel branch of hominid and not actually in our direct genetic line at all.

One of the upcoming chapters will discuss the genetics and biology of humanity in more detail, so let us not do it now. There are other mysteries to reveal.

There was nothing clearly laid down in the geological record that indicated a line of developing Homo Sapiens until about two hundred thousand years ago, and then suddenly, completely modern human phenotypes appeared from nowhere. Where did we come from?

Let us take a dip in the deep end of the pool of history, just to see how far it extends. About 4.55 billion years ago, our planet was formed as a flaming ball of magma in space. It took about two hundred million years to cool down the surface to the point where there were actually places cool enough to not cook immediately.

As soon as the planet formed, we got our fair share of comets bombarding the planet, delivering staggering amounts of water. For a long time, the water would stay flash vaporized into steam, making a hot atmosphere of various noxious chemicals and a lot of water vapor.

Sooner or later, the surface cooled enough for the water to rain down into what first became shallow seas, and eventually became substantial oceans. Almost as soon as the water was able to stay in liquid form, the first life appeared as one-celled prokaryotic cells. That was about 4.3 billion years ago.

It looks like life might have almost sputtered out on Earth several times, but then the evidence of its existence increased dramatically about 2.9 billion years ago. That was probably due to the terraforming that cyanobacteria did to the ecosystem and atmosphere.

Stromatolites are structures that the cyanobacteria

formed while generating oxygen in the first photosynthesis process in the earthly ecosystem. Shortly after the cyanobacteria appeared, they formed the first Eukaryotic cells by invading larger cells and feeding the host cells using their nifty photosynthesis in exchange for a place to stay. Life went on as just a bunch of one-celled things for a long time after that, until about six hundred million years ago, in fact.

From about 600 to about 400 million years ago, cells began to clump together into larger organisms. Some of the early ones were really alien looking, or perhaps just alien?

Earth developed basic fish, amphibians, and insects, along with all the non-flowering plant forms during this time, and it took a long time to get to every kid's favorite animals, the dinosaurs. You know the story after that, so let us skip to about 2.9 million years ago.

About 2.9 to 2.6 million years ago, the Earth started into its sixth major ice age, called the Quaternary ice age. We are still in that ice age today, although at some unknown position in what is known as an interglacial period, where the ice sheets have retreated for a time. Don't worry, they will be back.

Since the beginning of the Quaternary, the planet has been going through cycles of ice advancement and retreats, each cycle lasting a few thousand years. The previous ice ages have all lasted in the neighborhood of 100 million years or more each, so we will probably have severe problems with our breadbasket croplands several times over the next few million years, as the ice advances to cover the upper states.

According to common wisdom, our species has never known any climate other than that of ice age cycles. There have been at least three major migrations of humans over to North America in the last one hundred thousand years. Strangely enough, the first one was probably by water almost 70 thousand years ago, while the others were most likely migrations of opportunity across land bridges exposed by low ocean levels during the glacial periods.

If you go by the standard assumptions of our esteemed archeology and associated sciences, sometime about three or four thousand years before Christ, people changed from hunter-gatherers to tending crops, building cities and tending livestock. They waltz right on by some huge questions. I am going to list some of those questions now.

Even though there are major bits of evidence that Egypt rose to prominence well after the heyday of the Sumerian civilization, the world of archeology is run by Egyptologists. They could not have Egypt not be first, so they would have us believe that both empires existed during the same years.

They neglect the fact that physical evidence clearly shows that some of the true megalithic sites, such as the larger pyramids, the Sphinx, and even the far distant Stonehenge is obviously much older than anything that the Egyptians could have built, and probably not even the Sumerians were around when they were built.

Most of the Old Testament that both the Christians and the Hebrews revere was taken straight out of Sumer, including such details as the great flood. If you look at what the Sumerians wrote as fact instead of fiction (which is the tone of how they wrote it), then one of the transits of the weather from a glacial to an interglacial state caused a higher ocean level, which covered much of the populated areas of the world. Most of the human cities have always been located next to oceans and other waterways.

Modern science acknowledges but does not usually mention that the continents are surrounded by submerged cities in waters usually between 150 and 400 feet in depth. There are several hundred of these cities, ranging in sophistication and most of which test as being at least from that time frame of the end of the last glacial, somewhere about 10,500 BC.

To live in cities, the inhabitants could not be hunter-gatherers. They had to raise crops and livestock. That pushes back the time to practice those things so that the Sumerians did not have to invent a stupendous number of things all at the same time, but it still strains credulity.

Think about it. Agriculture and animal husbandry were established by 4500 BC, even if you ignore the sunken cities. This means that humans managed to selectively breed wild herd animals to be cows and sheep, wild wolves to become Lassie, and somehow, they had to coax several grains into tripling their DNA density and complexity, so that they were what we wanted them to be.

They had to do all of these things at once so that they could keep eating, and meanwhile, they were using huge stones that even our modern equipment cannot manipulate to build megalithic buildings for unknown purposes. Common sense tells us that people struggling for survival do not build megaliths. They build the simplest house they can use to do what they need them to do.

Somehow, ancient man did all of these things at once, if you believe what we are told. With no practice, they conceived of and built cities, modified the animals and plants around them into food and helper forms, and built monuments meant to last forever using unknown techniques that we cannot duplicate today. I have a hard time believing that we know the whole story.

As Paul Harvey used to say, it is time for the rest of the story. Actually, it is time to mention a couple of strange contradictions to show that the story may be far from complete.

The world is full of fossils, even though most events do not leave a fossil, so fossils are rare in comparison to events that have taken place. The point is that for every fossil you see, the event the fossil represents probably was duplicated millions of times without leaving a fossil.

One of the strange factoids in our geologic record is some fossils where human actions seem to have taken place at times where current science claims no humans existed. Usually, these are fossilized footprints in mud, which involved the fossilization of other native organics, proving the interaction. Sometimes, it is just fossilized human remains in strata when humans supposedly did not exist.

A man named William J. Meister discovered a fossilized footprint of what appeared to be a size 13 army boot crushing a trilobite while he was out looking for fossils in Utah, in 1968. Since trilobites went extinct over 250 million years ago, this means that someone stepped on one at least that long ago. Did someone invent time machines while I was focused on other things?

There are other anomalies out there to consider. There is a detailed and correct map of the continent of Antarctica, which shows features of the land that are not visible as long as the ice sheet covers the land.

This map has been around for a few centuries now, and nobody knows where it came from. The ice cap has covered the land since the beginning of the Quaternary Ice Age, more than two million years ago.

We can use modern technology to verify the true land features, but by any method, we believe that ancient man might have had, they would have to have seen the landscape without ice and had a point of view above the continent. Even with our technology, we have to fly over the land to sound for the covered features.

Even though the Egyptologists insist that Egypt was the first at everything, it is obvious that the history of civilization on Earth goes back a long way before Egypt, before even Sumer, even before the last glaciation made driving chariots a tricky winter sport. Major cities existed long before Sumer or Egypt.

There were civilizations in the ancient world that indisputably predated Egypt, such as India in the Indus Valley, China along the Yangtze River, and all of the aforementioned submerged cities. All indications are that the deeper we dig the further back in time we will find civilization to have existed.

There is a universal commonality to architecture. That commonality is the presence of one of the styles of pyramids, no matter where you look. It might be in the form of a stepped ziggurat, or in the more traditional smooth pyramids of Egypt.

One of the more puzzling aspects of ancient architecture is the size of the projects that the people took on. Most of the populations throughout history lived on the fine edge of starvation. One bad crop or one too many months of drought, and people were dying of hunger.

Because the average citizen of most previous civilizations has always lived so close to starvation, their efforts are usually aimed in a single-minded way at ensuring sufficient food for their survival. Such a mindset does not tend to produce people that will waste huge amounts of effort building massive stone structures when a small wooden one will provide just as much shelter and protection as the mega-structures.

The existence of massive stone structures creates a real question. Why would people expend enormous efforts and risk death to build these massive pyramids and other buildings? What could have been more important than survival?

There are only a couple of reasonable answers to that question. It could be that building the structures were seen to have more survival value than not to build them. This could be because the Rulers or the gods required these structures.

They also might have built the structures because it was easy to build them. Strangely enough, this might be a valid answer, because some of these structures are too big for our current technology to make. Since the ancients could build them, it suggests that they had access to something that was superior to our own technology.

The question of technology is a valid one. The metal orichalcum, which was reported as the metal used in Atlantis, and composed of zinc and copper, was recently found in a shipwreck. Since the refining of zinc is believed to have been accomplished only in the past thousand years, the metal suggests metal refinement techniques far beyond what is thought to have existed, so far back in time.

There are also anomalies in historical artifacts, such as meteor-steel bladed knives before man was supposed to be able to forge them, and battery urns from ancient Egypt. While these items are not part of architecture per se, they do point to the likelihood of advanced technology in history and in prehistory.

I think that we have amassed enough information to take the next step forward in our march to a consensus conclusion about the question of alien life. In the next chapter, we will spend a few words to state what we think we know so far, and then we will continue the trip into the twisted places that logic can lead us.

8 FIRST ASSUMPTION

We have come a short way into the mystery that is the question of alien life. Our question is really a set of questions, and they go something like this. Does life exist anywhere else in the universe other than Earth, and is there any other intelligent life? If they exist, do any of these intelligent aliens come to Earth to visit us?

We have common sense observation, Occam's razor and Recursive Anthropic Principle tools to keep us on our course. When any naughty little concepts start causing us trouble, we can quickly beat them into submission before saddling them up for a ride to Jellystone Park.

Our observation of the life process here on our planet and the nebulous but undeniable math of Drake's equation tells us that life must exist in all possible forms throughout the universe unless we are completely wrong about the nature of reality. The RAP tells us that the universe we live in is not as twisted as it would have to be to be a dead universe, and Occam's razor tells us that the universe is a place where life abounds, and where many examples of hominoid alien life are reported to visit the Earth.

We are willing to accept that aliens are visiting Earth. We have not worked out why they all seem to be hominoid in form, but it is starting to look a little like a family deal.

With Drake's equation in hand, we know beyond a reasonable doubt that the opportunity for life abounds throughout the universe. Unless we want to commit the sin of hubris, we must assume that there is nothing unusual about life on Earth. This also implies that there is nothing to stop life from arising everywhere and from all of these cradles of life. There is not any reason to doubt that intelligent life is springing up everywhere.

If this alien life arises in other star systems, then some very hard technology is required to bridge that gulf between the stars. Let us assume that these visitations from other star systems are indeed taking place, and move on to a more interesting question.

In any reports of alien contact where the alien bodies formats are reported that I know about, all of the aliens reported have been either hominoid or an Analog of hominoid. By an Analog, I mean that they are described as bipedal with human symmetry, actions, and behaviors.

The type of alien reported most are the 'Greys,' which you most likely know well since you are reading this book. Others are the more human-like 'Nordics,' or the 'Reptilians' (description based on superficial scales), along with lots of other hominoids. There is no Cosmic Octopi, and no 'Starfish from the stars.'

There have been some descriptions of insectoid aliens, but if you examine the reported body forms carefully, it resembles a human evolving toward insectoid more than it resembles a parallel evolution of insects toward a human format. In other words, it seems to me that there is some relationship between all reported aliens visiting us, and humanity.

There are two obvious reasons why only hominoid aliens might visit us here on our human planet. The aliens could be operating from a galaxy-wide prime directive, or they could indeed be related to humanity. Let us try to figure out which of these is the more likely answer.

There are over a hundred prime amino acids that are fine building blocks for any life form. On Earth, only twenty of these amino acids are required to ingest for making baby Earth-spawn, with another two forms used to build rather exotic proteins in the cells. Minor alterations of the prime twenty are characteristic of Earth, and life forms using some other amino acids might as well be yelling that they are alien.

The wildcard in the structures of amino acids is the R group carbons. You can tell if life arose here on Earth because life here uses these 20 primary amino acids, even though on alien worlds, there would be virtually no chance that life would develop using the same twenty amino acids.

The strange thing about our alien visitors is that they seem strongly interested in our biology. They are always busy doing incomprehensible medical tests on Earth Life, ending of course with the unforgettable anal probe.

It is virtually unquestionable that the genetic material in our bodies is the same as the genetic material in their bodies since they are so taken with it. The question is why?

The possibility of all aliens visiting Earth sharing the same body plan as humanity is virtually zero, unless either there is a universal human body plan for all Earth area aliens, or non-hominoid aliens have no interest in visiting. It could also be that every alien we see is a robotic mockup along a hominoid format, following some universal 'don't tell the natives' prime directive.

It could also be that all of the aliens that decide to visit are actually related to us. If we can figure out how that might be possible, it would go a long way to explaining the rather bizarre fixation that the aliens seem to have on human genetics and biology.

I can sit down for a half hour and come up with a dozen better designs for intelligent aliens to embody than the human plan. The idea that all interested local aliens are hominoid is ridiculous.

The fact that they are all reported as hominoid makes it feasible that the human form is a disguise so as not to alarm the locals. This could be an intergalactic prime directive. Let us discuss the reasons for and against that idea.

The most obvious problem with that idea is why they would create crudely hominoid masks, such as the Greys, instead of masks that we Earthlings could not distinguish from local humans? From the abilities reported, it is obvious that the aliens could make humans believe that they were only interacting with another human.

The same logic applies if the bodies are robotic instead of protoplasmic. If the objective is to hide the alien nature of the visitors, they are not doing a credible job. Occam's razor says that is not likely what is happening.

We are back to the idea that maybe all interested aliens are hominoid because that is the only phenotype that works, or because all of the aliens we see are related to each other, and perhaps to us as well. To believe that the human form is the only form that aliens can successfully evolve into is an idea that is so beyond reasonable that believing it is a belief in divine meddling at a level that negates all meaning in our own existence.

I think that we can discount the idea that we possess the one and only acceptable form for intelligent life, and assume that we are attracting only human-shaped aliens to come to visit us. I do not know about your family life, but that sounds a lot like family behavior to me.

I grew up in a small town, and everybody knew everybody. You could expect to be visited by just about anyone in the town since you were not a stranger. You would expect to, but most of the time, it was still your cousins, or aunts, or some other relatives that paid you a visit. The others just came by if they had some business that required it.

I grant you that the aliens could still be here to analyze truly alien genetics that recreates the human body on Earth, but somehow, the aliens have been reported to produce alien-human hybrids with the Earth Women. I guess Earth women are easy after all!

No matter how easy it is, I do not think that aliens cover light years to play doctor with humans to no purpose. Something about human existence, genetics, and biology keep them coming back. Allow me to speculate.

If humans have been in basically modern form for roughly two hundred thousand years, why is it that we only see technological advancements of significance in the last ten thousand years? Could it be that everything that we have been doing has already been done at least once in prehistory?

Could it be that humanity has developed the technology before to leave the Earth, to travel among the planets, and eventually travel to the near stars? Perhaps what we see as aliens are just our descendants coming back to visit their long-lost family homes, and make sure that their backward family members are surviving.

With science at its current level in genetics, nanotechnology, physics, and the rest of the disciplines, how long would it take for the forms of humanity to change drastically to adjust to a universe of needs? I do not think that it would take more than a couple thousand years for star-faring humans to change their bodies into forms more alien than any of the reported forms.

A wonderful science fiction writer named Stephen Baxter describes the rise of a Terran Empire, fighting against a foe called the Xeelee. In a matter of a few thousand years, in an environment involving both defeats and victories, humanity changes into several forms, from essentially hive mentalities to multiple coded, and into every possible change to suit different environments you can imagine. With technology, the changes would not take much time.

There are so many conclusions that can be easily ruled out, such as there is no apparent invasions or genocides taking place, so of the likely scenarios, we can put together a tentative assumption. In this context, an assumption is the conclusion of a smaller argument. This is the rough idea.

What we are seeing as aliens are actually human-related species. They originated on Earth, or on an alternate Earth. I will explain that later.

They probably are the descendants of humanity from several thousand years ago, humans who left Earth and changed to suit their new environments. It is possible that they came more recently from an Earth that is generated from the quantum nature of our universe. Whatever it is, they are related to us.

I know that some of you might consider the assumption just described to be way too unlikely for it to be simple enough to pass Occam's razor. It is not as complicated as it seems.

Imagine that I have a thousand dollars hidden in my house in a community where nobody else hides money in their house. I tell ten people about my money. Burglary is rare in my community.

I come home one day, and the house has been broken into. Someone appears to have walked straight back to the one spot that I described to my friends where I hid my money, and took the money. Nothing else was disturbed.

Even though I live in a community of several thousand people, the crime suggests that the criminal had prior knowledge of where the money was located, and suspicion rests heavily on the ten people I told or someone they told.

On the alien argument, we have previously decided that we must assume that what we think we see is really what we see, and we see lots of hominoid aliens flying around in their high tech vehicles. We do not see any non-hominoid aliens. We do not believe that any galactic prime-directive could be so effectively followed that all members of all galactic civilizations could so effectively pretend to be hominoid without any accidental reveals.

We must decide that the similarity between what they appear to be and what we are must be part of the reason that the aliens are focusing their attention on us. The accumulation of things that the 'aliens' are doing, such as interbreeding and medical actions tell us that the aliens are not alien at all since they appear to have the genetics of earthly origin.

Occam's razor tells us that the reason why the 'aliens' look so much like us is that they are related to us. The Recursive Anthropic Principle finds that to be an acceptable conclusion to reach. Unless someone finds the evidence to falsify this new assumption, let us use it to build our central argument.

9 ANCIENT CIVILIZATIONS

We do not have as much information as we might wish of human civilization earlier than about three thousand years ago. Even the origin of Abraham is obscured by the mists of time. Few realize that the father of the Hebrew nation was originally a war captain of sorts in service of the Akkadian empire. The first Semitic Akkadian people had invaded the original Sumerians about a thousand years before that time. Abraham was a citizen of the Akkadian-Sumerian empire.

We have archeological evidence of much earlier settlements that support hints and references from historical documents. It is time to spin a tapestry of those things that have recently come to light.

As I mentioned before, there are hundreds of sunken cities just off the shore of most of the continents of Earth. They are at depths of one-hundred-fifty to four hundred feet deep, suggesting that they were built when the oceans were slightly more than four hundred feet lower than they are today.

This suggests that the cities were built sometime during the glacial period of the ice age, when more water was locked away inside of glaciers, reducing the water levels of the oceans. We have since come into an interglacial warming trend.

Our own cities are built at nearly ocean level when close to the oceans. Since they have been built during the late part of a warming period, they will probably find themselves inconveniently far from the ocean during the next glacial period.

The cities just discussed were submerged about 11 to 12 thousand years ago, although there may be some of them that date back to the last interglacial, about 25 to 28 thousand years ago. There is some evidence of mega structures and cities from a time before this.

In Southernmost Africa, there is an area in Zimbabwe in which several million strange stone structures have been found. They were thought to be habitats or burial sites for a long while, but they were not built with doors or other means to access them. It is almost as though they were some sort of sound based energetic system.

Throughout the area, there are gigantic aqueducts, used by the locals as cattle trails. Nobody knows why such a megastructure site exists. There would be irrigation enough to feed the entire ancient world, and we have already discussed why it is insane to build hard stone structures if you are at starvation levels of existence.

One strong hint is that there are hundreds of small

ancient gold mines in the area, dating from a time when gold should not have been that sought after. Conservative estimates of the age of the gold mines, and the structures place them at perhaps 20,000 years old, and bolder estimates place them at over 200,000 years old. Who wanted gold back then, and what stores existed where you could spend the gold?

There is Lore confirmation of the existence of this site as an extremely influential ancient mining operation. Other caches of lore mention the ancient advanced continent island of Atlantis, along with other lesser-known ancient civilizations that modern science has long scoffed at, but that seems more and more likely to have existed after all.

Recently there has been a rapid-fire series of discoveries of Megalithic structures found in Ukraine. They appear to date from 20,000 to as much as 30,000 years ago, and the language and culture recorded on the artifacts suggest that this might be the civilization from which the Sumerians descended. The writing is a kind of proto-Sumerian. The symbology shown on artifacts contains common symbology with the Sumerian, Egyptian, and Hindu cultures.

Just as in Sumer, Egypt, and many other places all over the world, there have been pyramidal structures discovered in this Ukrainian culture, called the Aratta Empire. Backtracking to other cultures, it is evident that Aratta had influence that reached all through Europe, Asia, and Africa, and even around the world.

One excavated city of the Aratta that you may have heard of has the name Gobeki Tepi. It is located in the area of Turkey, implying that Aratta was much more expansive than one might have thought. As far as we know, it only went back to the last glacial period, but it is still thousands of years older than the most ancient estimate of civilization believed to be valid only a decade ago.

We do not know how far humanity has reached in the past, but we can make some good guesses. If humanity has been at fundamentally the same level of potential for the last 200,000 years, it hardly seems likely that every advancement of humans has been achieved only in the last ten thousand years.

It seems likely that mankind has risen and fallen many times since we developed, and there is a likelihood that we have achieved modern levels of accomplishment more than once. If our own civilization fell, it would be hard to uncover evidence for high tech after a couple of centuries, and almost impossible in a thousand years. Add to that a bias against the possibility, and it might never be recognized.

The next couple of chapters will touch on civilizations that feature much evidence of possible alien influence. After that, we will get around to dissecting some fact rich subjects to continue to prove our arguments.

10 SUMERIAN

Any serious student of myths that suggest alien visitors to Earth are real must start with the ancient kingdom of Sumer. There are several reasons why they are the prime starting point. One of the biggest reasons to look at them is that they state right out that aliens, which we usually interpret as their gods, visited them, and gave them the knowledge that they possessed.

At least by 4500 BC, and most likely a lot earlier than that, the Sumerian people came out of nowhere, fully equipped with city building using heavy stones, and astronomical information firmly in hand that required space flight or powerful telescopes to obtain it. The Sumerians referred to the Anunnaki not as gods, but as their wise mentors.

As you know, different people have different personalities. Whole cultures of peoples may have a particular temperament, making for distinctive behaviors. The Sumerians wrote in a 'just the facts, ma'am' sort of style. The best-known book of Sumerian 'fiction' is The Chronicles of Gilgamesh, and it is in a style that I can best describe as a private journal written in an unusual poetic style.

Most of what the Sumerians wrote was bills of laden, and even the stuff they wrote that wasn't business was written in that same matter of fact style. I do not think that they actually worshipped gods in the way we might worship. I think the Sumerians saw them more like the big guys with the answers. Think of them as the football hero, if the hero had the answer to every question you really wanted to have answered.

The creation myth in Sumer says that the gods came to our world to secure a lot of gold. Sitchin said that the gold was intended to repair the atmosphere of the homeworld of the gods. I personally think that the gods were just greedy. The homeworld of the gods is described as having an extreme hyperbolic orbit around the sun, and I think that it is unlikely that anyone could survive the colder parts of that cycle.

The gods were supposedly mining gold here on Earth. They got tired of doing the work, and they finally talked their head gods into making some mini-Anunnaki to do the work for them. They decided that it was time to just veg out and let the minions do the work.

After a few thousand years of work, Enki created a mated pair of suitable specimens of the proper minions. Since the gods are not prejudiced, it did not take long before the newly formed humans were cooking, cleaning, mining, and tending the crops, and then the pretty girls got to slide into the god's beds at night.

As the population of humans grew, the Anunnaki spread the species everywhere on the Earth. I personally think that the big guys came here to enjoy lording it over the world. They just liked gold and slaves, and they all wanted to be the king.

Generally speaking, the Anunnaki were described as between seven and nine feet tall, with six fingers on each hand, and six toes on each foot. They were disgustingly white, which might explain why so many of the ancient people thought that the first white people they saw must be the gods returning.

The women were slightly smaller than the males. It was not well explained, but it looks to me as though the fertility between male and female was not as high as you would think it should be, and it may have been higher in a human-Anunnaki coupling.

In addition to founding the ancient cities in the Middle East, the Anunnaki have been credited with establishing other cities all over the world, including North and South America, the ancient mythical lands of Atlantis and Lumeria, and the Empire of Rama in the Indus region.

According to the Sumerians, the Anunnaki have been messing around here on Earth for 430,000 years. An unknown amount of time, but certainly more than 10,000 years were spent interacting with humanity. Hundreds of the cities that have been submerged after the last glacial age ended were created by or for the Anunnaki.

We can be fairly sure that space-faring entities actually

did interact with the Sumerians because of a cartouch correctly describing the Solar System that appears on one of their mosaics, which would require technology equivalent to planetary travel to render.

Here is what we know about the alien gods so far. They were larger than human, with six digits per limb. Their skin was white enough for them to be identified as gods by that color.

The Anunnaki were ambitious and greedy, and they saw themselves as the proper Rulers of the Kingdom. They frequently fought among themselves for various reasons, and the wars between the towns probably were just proxy wars for the squabbles between the gods.

Zacharia Sitchin's translations of ancient Sumerian text tell of the existence of the gods. They were the descendants of Anu (Sky), and the term Anunnaki means either the descendants of Anu or 'those who came down from the Sky.'

According to Lore, the Anunnaki are responsible for the creation of Man, along with the introduction of technology. The Anunnaki arrived on Earth about 430 thousand years ago, and created humanity to mine gold for them, and serve as the servants and occasional bedmates for the gods. They also built cities in Africa to service the mining operations, and the cities of the Sumer Empire to process the cargo, and serve as spaceports.

Wherever the Anunnaki went, they built cities, they ruled the cities, and frequently they went to war with other cities. As we will describe in the next chapter, they created the city of Atlantis and the Rama Empire, and the two great empires fought each other around 10,000 years ago. I think that we had two losers of that war.

They were responsible for having us measure time and distance in multiples of six, such as minutes and hours, and inches and feet. They contributed the gene for red hair to the human species, along with an absurd desire for gold and an excess of strange genetic anomalies.

The strangest thing about the gods is how consistently they are described in every pantheon of gods around the world. They are always oversized, ambitious and unruly, prone to violence and drama.

When we drag our trusty Occam's razor out to check the Anunnaki out, we discover that there is much evidence that supports the idea of some contact that contributed to our creation and the advancement of human tech. It was willful and capricious, and consistent from culture to culture. In fact, it was so consistent that it is simpler to accept the idea that they were real than to explain them away. As we will show later, just the biological evidence alone comes as close to proof of their existence as one is ever likely to get nowadays.

11 RAMAN EMPIRE

We have plenty of evidence that there have been cities and mega structures on this planet for many centuries. If you include such sites as Gobeki Tepi and the rest of the Aratta sites, you can easily see the age of human civilization cast back from ten to twenty thousand years at a minimum. If you add in the ambiguous but strange mining-related sites in South Africa, you are talking about hundreds of thousands of years to consider.

The oldest sites that we can see a flurry of confirmatory evidence for is the Aratta Empire civilization. These involve the oldest confirmed written language, the oldest located states that are referred to in outside documentation, and a broad assortment of physical artifacts.

The land that is now known as Atlantis, and that which is now known to us as the Rama Empire coexisted with Aratta. They may have even have existed a few years before Aratta, although that is by no means verified.

When one is tracking down the historical existence of a

legendary city or civilization, such as Troy or Atlantis, it is considered important that the target site is mentioned by other ancient cultures as real existing places. That is a little like establishing a backlink for your website to establish its legitimacy.

When Plato mentioned the existence of Atlantis reported to him by a single priest, it was not enough to make it more than a myth. When the ancient Vedas of India chronicled the battle of the forces of the Rama Empire against the invading Asvin aircraft more than ten thousand years ago, this is helpful in confirming the reality of the place now known as Atlantis.

The Vedas are books of prose that preserved knowledge for the Indus people. They tell of the ancient wars of gods and men using the flying machines called Vimanas. The gods had taught men to make and fly these aircraft, and they were used in an ancient war on both sides when the people from Atlantis attacked Rama.

The area that was the center of the Rama Empire was actually located just north of India in Pakistan. This was the area of the Indus Valley that contained the ancient city of Mohenjo-Daro.

In the war of Asvin and Rama, the Atlantean Valakri flying craft began a bombardment of the Rama homeland, attempting to crush the Rama Vimana armada before they could get off the ground. Although Atlantis inflicted heavy damage, the Rama fleet managed to go on the offensive.

There are two sides to any conflict. Usually, it is the winner's side that gets reported as the 'good guys,' but shortly after the war, the land of Atlantis went under the sea, so the only record we have left of this conflict by direct participants was the record of the Rama Empire. They claim that they were the peaceful ones, and Atlantis was the bad people.

At any rate, it is written in the Vedas that the Atlantean and Rama Empires fought between ten and twelve thousand years ago, and the Rama Empire ultimately lost. The more skeptical among us might discount the tale of the war as a work of fiction, just as they believed the story of Troy was fiction until they finally found the city.

Modern Western science has tended to discount the validity of the Veda's account of the Empire of Rama. It was not until recently that some interesting evidence has come to light to support the idea that the tale of Rama was true.

The Veda's described a war conducted from aircraft, using weapons that sound suspiciously like lasers and nuclear weapons. Just north of India in Pakistan, the ruins of an ancient city called Mohenjo-Daro tells an ancient and terrifying tale.

Mohenjo-Daro appears to have become a city of the dead in an instant. A great deal of sudden damage was part of its demise, and everywhere, there is evidence that the people close in suffered death in a matter of seconds, while outliers may have taken days to die.

There are some tales of the shadows of people being flash burned onto the masonry of the city, A Geiger counter will reveal a very high radioactive count, and there are sections of the ground in the area that is covered in the slightly greenish plate-like glass that is characteristic of nearby nuclear explosions.

Mohenjo-Daro has been the site of several short-term excavations. Digs in this field were started and shut down. This was due to excessive radiation found on the remains of humans found in the area.

The radioactive glass and human remains found in the area around Mohenjo-Daro, along with the many submerged cities around the world, suggest the existence of a very high civilization at the end of the last glacial age. This could be purely a human achievement, but it could also be the result of the alien interaction that the ancients claimed happened.

The evidence suggests a timeline that may explain some of the blank spots in our history. Let us start with meddlesome aliens along the lines of the Anunnaki, and take it from there.

At some point in the distant past, it is reasonable to assume that intelligent aliens might have tinkered with our genes to help us improve, or maybe just to entertain them. Either these aliens were hominoid, or they predate any record of what they looked like.

Most thinking people can admit that human civilization tends to occur in cycles. Someone gets an opportunity or a hot idea, and they spark a new culture into existence. The new culture will build on any available knowledge base quickly. Eventually, the culture will hit a snag, such as invasion or a natural disaster, which will kick them back into the dark ages until someone starts the cycle all over again.

Nobody knows how many times humanity has reached the technological level of today, and then be driven back to the Stone Age, only to start it all over again. Roughly twelve thousand years ago was the last time that that cycle occurred worldwide, which corresponded with the end of the glacial period, and what may have been a relatively rapid rise of ocean levels as the ice sheets release their trapped water. After that, a lot of cities were under the waves.

Since the flood, humanity has been digging its way out of ignorance. We are near to the point where we can send a few of us to seed the stars. How many times might humanity have been to that same point over the last 200,000 years?

If humanity devotes itself to living on other worlds, one of the most obvious things that we might do is to modify ourselves to make it easier for us to suit the environments. This would leave the star-born as many strange variations of the human form, perhaps even having scales, gray or bigheaded.

I am not saying that this is what happened, but the modified bodies of star-born humans would probably look *exactly* like the aliens we read about in the reports. We cannot know if the Progenitor aliens that created us were actually hominoid as well, but so many 'modern' aliens are hominoid that it cannot be a coincidence.

Let us take the simplest approach, and set up a simple timeline. I will state a series of events, and we can debate them later on in this book.

Life arose on Earth close to 4.3 billion years ago. It could have been spontaneous, or it could have been Panspermia. Life went through all of those transformations that we know of and love over the eons until finally, primates appeared on the planet.

A few hundred thousand years ago, intelligent super-humans that the Sumerians called the Anunnaki appeared on Earth, using advanced technology. For whatever reason you choose to believe, they needed assistants, and they created humanity to be those assistants.

From the fact that humans and Anunnaki produced children, we have to conclude that the Anunnaki were definitely of Earthly origin, and closely related to humanity. Even if the Anunnaki replaced all of our genes with Anunnaki genes, the biocompatibility between our species means that the life that became Anunnaki originated in our oceans.

This suggests that the Anunnaki were earthly transplants to the stars, and they came home to uplift their brethren, or they actually never left Earth. If they are transplants, then there are only three possibilities that I can imagine.

Perhaps there were earlier Progenitor gods who tweaked the Anunnaki to create an original, intelligent creature and took them with them to other planets and stars as servants. The Anunnaki may also have been an earlier iteration of advanced hominoid, who left the planet and came back, to pay it forward by creating smart slaves for themselves. The third possibility is that the Anunnaki is the Analog of humanity from a parallel Earth, and they found a way to enter our universe to colonize our version of the planet.

Nobody knows which version of the arrival of aliens is the true one, but they are all fascinating to think about. I threw the parallel world idea in the mix for completeness. We will get around to explaining it in more detail in a future chapter.

12 ORIGINS

We have decided that the simplest answer that fits all the facts about aliens is that they exist, they visit us on a regular basis and for some reason, all of the ones we see seem to be hominoids. None of these things *has* to be true, but Occam's razor tells us that it is more likely than most of the other more deceptive solutions to the puzzle.

Now we are at that point where we probe the question of origin. Specifically, what is the origin of these hypothetical aliens that all the kids these days seem to see? Just because they are stranger than most of your neighbors does not mean that they come from another star system. It could be the perfectly normal-seeming Uncle Ted type that lives two doors down that comes from Arcturus.

It is reasonable that the aliens we sometimes get reports about are actual star travelers. To make the trip, they would need robust technology that is able to protect the vehicle at extreme speeds from impacts with rocks and asteroids of all sorts in their path. They would also need to exceed the speed of light or to be able to travel at speeds approaching the speed of light. This would allow the aliens to make the trip within an objectively reasonable time, or allow them to take advantage of time dilation effects to shorten the time they experience for them to make the trip.

The aliens also could create giant generation ships, and spend their lives traveling to planets that their children might see in their lifetimes. If aliens are not as impatient as we are, this may well be the way they prefer to travel.

Given the reported flight characteristics of alien craft, I suspect that most of our visitors would indeed be capable of high velocity sub-light or possibly faster than light travel, so it is likely that those are the ways they would travel. I strongly suspect that most species wishing to use generation ships that could complete an interstellar trip would probably just install a space drive on their planet, and travel in comfort to visit the neighbors.

It is also possible that the aliens come to our fair planet from somewhere within our own Solar System. This would make the requirements for the travel technology a little less robust, but it would carry other problems in its wake.

With travel distances less extended, the aliens could keep the spaceship speeds down to reasonable levels. You know what they say. When you solve one problem, another one will jump up into your lap.

Reports of alien-human interactions suggest that the aliens are quite comfortable in an earthly environment. When we look out into the Solar System, we do not see many places in the system that have an Earth-like environment.

I sort of doubt the idea that the aliens we see come from any of the other planets in the system, although they could have a very comfortable asteroid or moon that they have hollowed out to live in. A species could live in style with a crib like that!

The aliens we see could be coming from either planetary or interstellar space but originate from Earth in the distant past. They could also come from some place on or in Earth that humans do not ordinarily see. That would make them as validly as for us of being Native-Terrestrials.

My interpretation of Occam's razor suggests that the most likely answer to the origin problem is that humanity has been at high technology levels before in the past, and during one or more of these civilizations established space colonies and populations. In this case, the 'aliens' would be returnees to the world of their origin.

What if the aliens are from Earth, but they are not *from* Earth? One of the interpretations of quantum mechanics that successfully answers the question of what happens to all of those possible outcomes in events is called the Many Worlds Theory.

The Many Worlds Theory says that every possible outcome of every event is real in an infinitely branching multiverse. For every universe where you turned right, another version of you turned left. Endless variations of humanity exist on endless shadow earths, and some of them must occasionally discover how to visit nearby probable

Earths.

In some of these parallel Earths, the species might be much changed, with events speeding up changes in a manner that would make that world resemble a world of the distant future or even the distant past. This is one way that we can have effective time travel, even if you do not believe in the possibility of time travel.

For those of you who believe that time travel is possible, I submit that the alien hominoids that are reported to visit us could be visitors from the future. If you believe in former iterations of humanity on Earth, they could even be visitors from the past!

Unless you believe that all aliens are hominoid in shape, the set of origins mentioned so far covers your basic alien origin. One origin not yet mentioned which is possible, but in my mind unlikely, is a visitation by an uncharacteristically empathic machine culture.

A machine culture may be the remaining AI entities from a defunct or extinct biological creator species, which might still have interests in exploring the galaxy around them. I would ordinarily expect a machine culture to examine our world using nanotechnologies so I would not expect us to ever know that they were looking at us.

If for some reason the machine wishes us to see them, they might indeed create robotic or even biological bodies for themselves that mimic us. I do not believe this is happening here though, as I think that the machines would create bodies indistinguishable from humans if they even announced themselves with a macro body at all.

So there you have it. We have just discussed the most likely origins for the hominoid aliens that are commonly reported to visit us. You already know what answer I suspect is the correct one.

We will be coming back to each of these possible origin scenarios in future chapters, but for now, we will analyze the genetic links that we might share with the alien visitors in the next chapter. This will be closely followed by a chapter that questions how alien technology can make its way to our planet, but then succumb to earthly forces, causing crashes and other 'accidental' sharing of technology.

13 GENETICS

Somebody tinkered with us. There, I have said it. There is indisputable evidence that some of our traits, biology, and genetics required the intervention of something that was striving to bring about intentional changes to us.

To show this fact, I will need to point out the features of other organisms that will provide a good baseline for indicating how clearly our own characteristics have been modified. I will be pulling much of this information from the pages of the book EVERYTHING YOU KNOW IS WRONG by Lloyd Pye and from the minds of Lloyd Pye and Zecharia Sitchin.

The book is fantastic, and I wholeheartedly suggest that you pick up a copy of the book and read it as soon as possible. Pye covers a range of subjects dealing with the origin of humans and humanity's relationship to the rest of the life forms on Earth.

We will be going over a half dozen or so of the most

glaring issues with humans that is evidence of tinkering, and unlikely if only evolution was responsible. If we consider an omnipotent and spiritual god to be responsible, then we must assume that such an entity made mistakes. That seems unlikely, so let us only consider gods with the little G for now.

I am going to believe that most of my dear readers believe in evolution as the engine of change for our cute little animal species. There are two parts to the typical actions of evolution.

When a species has a viable population, a small subset of that population will have small mutations, or differences, from its fellow kin. Most mutations are not useful for survival, and the mutant soon dies. Occasionally, the mutation is useful, and the mutant lives a long life, producing a large number of progeny before its death.

Everyone has an inherited mutation that makes them just a tad different from the rest of their fellows. The environment or even other creatures can pick and choose preferred features, creating a radically changed creature from tiny differences over a short span of time spent selecting for certain traits. Such traits as skin or hair color, physical features, and mental and emotional features can all be changed over relatively short periods of time.

Most of the changes to a species are of this sort. Small differences grow more modified over time, selecting for traits, which improve the survivability of the subject.

Some of these changes might be sexual traits, such as enlarged breasts, or they might be height, or skin or eye colors. Generally, the direction of change will be directed towards those traits most viable to survival.

If the environment is making the conditions, then the traits will tend directly toward the traits of strength, skills, or physical abilities that contribute to survival. If another creature is making the rules, such as when we breed dogs, then the results may not always point toward traits that seem to be survival values.

Turning a wolf into a lapdog does not appear to be of survival value at first glance until you factor in the wish of the breeder to have a lapdog. Then those traits become very pro-survival for the wolf turned dog.

All of this is just to point out that the direction of survival can be set by either environment or by an entity trying to breed in certain traits into the species. I bring this to the front for you to consider since there are many indications that entities rather than the environment have imposed some of our traits on us.

According to popular science, good old Homo Sapiens, in the form of Cro-Magnon man came into being 200,000 years ago, and at about 10,000 years ago, the species spontaneously changed into the modern form of human, which is basically the same form, but weaker. Also about 10,000 years ago, humans managed to make domesticated cows, sheep, and dogs out of the wild forms of the species, in what appeared to be overnight.

Humans also are assumed to have modified many crop plants overnight, causing them to be more nutritious and more complicated genetically. It is kind of hard to imagine how humans could have selectively modified plants so quickly into their modern forms.

According to Sitchin's version of what the Sumerians reported as history, Anu and the Anunnaki came to Earth 430,000 years ago and set about mining gold as a means of fixing the atmosphere of their homeworld. After a while, they got bored and asked Enki to create Anunnaki-like servants to do the work for them.

After a few thousands of years of experimentation, Enki managed to invent Humanity, and they became the servants of the gods in the mines, in the cities, and in the beds of the gods. I do not know how closely this reported history follows actual events, but if any part of it is true, then I think some of the answers about the human condition will fall into place.

It is remarkable how many things are wrong with the human anatomy. We are prone to diseases and malnutrition that no objective evolution should have allowed. Let us go through a list of these discrepancies.

Our feet are badly suited for the savanna landscape movement that we are supposedly designed to complete. We can see the grasping musculature of the tree-dwelling primate inherent in our feet, but the placement of the points of maximum load, and the appropriate force distributions are all wrong for what our feet are supposed to successfully complete.

The fact is that our ankles and the leg bones that couple into the ankle should be moved slightly forward on the foot, so that the load is centered on the foot, and the weight is distributed more equally. The backbone has been curved into an s-shape to allow the upright walking position to happen while maintaining the function of the rest of the body processes.

Unlike all other primates and all reported hominoid walking methods, the human walking process involves rotation around the hip structure, locking and unlocking of the leg at the knee in the midpoint of the step, and a generally vast waste of energy and a high likelihood of damage. Instead of knee locks and hip rotations, the primates do not over-extend the leg into the lock position, and they do not waste the excess motion and increase the damage due to the hip rotations.

Much of the structure of the human body is subject to damage due to a far lower strength level than it was originally designed to have. For some unknown reason, when our species obtained a higher reasoning ability, it also lost the original primate strength.

The loss of the primate strength is a very perplexing mystery. When an organism is undergoing a change due to a new mutation, such as intelligence, the organism usually retains all of the other valuable assets they possess.

There is no reason why humans would have lost primate strength when they gained intelligence. A smart, strong human would be better than a smart, weak human.

It makes no sense for humans to have universally lost all of that strength in a normal evolutionary process. If an entity were the cause of the change, then the desire of the entity to eliminate the strength of the humans would act as a survival factor, and the loss of the strength would start to make sense after all.

If any members of homo sapiens had retained the original primate strength, the genes would have eventually won primacy in the bloodlines along with competitive intelligence. As long as the trait was not entirely expunged from the bloodlines, it is such a valuable trait that eventually, it must return to primacy in terms of characteristics of the species.

Breast size and other sexual characteristics in the females tend to exaggerated proportions beyond functionality. This is one set of traits that I could see as either being imposed on the species or is a matter of natural selection by prospective mates in the species itself.

Humans have an amazing inability to create the C, D, and E vitamins, along with a whole host of other necessary nutrient requirements for life. Most animals can produce any of these substances they need.

It is interesting to note that our inability to produce these substances is most closely similar to that of White Lab Rats, which have been genetically altered to most easily study such deficiencies. It could be that this lack was an intentional attempt to control the human subjects, or just shoddy work on the part of the creator entity.

Out of all of the animals that we have domesticated, only the dog has developed such an attachment to their humans that it falls somewhere between regarding the human as a super alpha pack leader, and worship. The only other animal on Earth which seems to share this same level of attachment to another being is humanity, which shows this same level of attachment to whatever form of 'god' they worship.

If you have ever noticed a truly feral dog, they carry a high sense of desperation in their actions. You can feel a cloud of despair from them because something they need and crave is missing from their lives. Without a human in their life, the dog's life is no longer complete.

We selected dogs with increasing dependencies on us. Something obviously did the same thing to us, causing the strange mental activity that we label 'worship.' Notice that nothing else seems to have developed this strange fixation to another species of creature. Is there any real doubt that this trait was bred into the species?

There are parts of the Sumerian lore that I suspect is in error. The planet that the Anunnaki came from is supposedly in a highly elliptical orbit around our sun. Such an orbit would result in a climate that was far too cold for life to survive for much of its path, so I doubt that the Anunnaki intended the gold they sought to repair the atmosphere of a doomed planet.

Most likely, the Anunnaki just wanted to set themselves up with their own private kingdoms, complete with willing subjects and all the gold and partying that they could stand. That seems to be what all of the activity appears to have delivered to them.

One of the problems with the modern opinion of the development of modern man into the city-dwelling crop raisers from the hunter-gatherer's tribes is the speediness of the process. Modern science would still have you believe that the transition, with the development of crops, cattle, dogs, and relatively modern society came about within a matter of about two thousand years or less, and without assistance.

One of the strange things about humans is that one of our chromosomes is actually a combination of the number two and number three chromosomes that exist in all of the other primate species. It is glued together in a manner that is not easy to explain, making us the only hominoid or hominid with 23 pairs of chromosomes instead of 24.

Mostly our genes are repeats and modifications of other genes found in the primate families, but there are 243 unique genes in the human genome, which are found nowhere else on Earth. Where did they come from?

Finally, of all of the species on our planet, we have the dubious honor of having the highest percentage of our genome screwed up to the point where we exhibit more genetic diseases than any other species. While many species have diabetes, cancer, and other genetically related diseases, only humanity has these diseases in such overwhelming numbers.

While any one or two of these conditions and data could be the result of mundane cause and effect evolution, the list of all of the data begs us to consider some interference with our development. Occam's razor tells us that the simplest explanation that explains all of these details is that we have been modified by an outside agency. Nothing else makes sense.

In the next chapter, we are going to take a look at an inconsistency. I consider it odd that aliens can travel from one star to another, but once they get here, they cannot keep from crashing their flying saucers. We are going to take a look at that, and see if we can come up with a better answer.

14 CRASHES

Our little Grey buddies fly their little flying saucers all the way here from Zeta Reticuli without a mishap, only to crash in various fields and woods all over our fair planet. The closest equivalent to that that I can think of is if you have a Pit Bull that is a consistent winner of many dogfights that is consistently beaten by your Chihuahua at home.

There is something that is too overt about the way those little spaceships crash so easily. One of those things went down in Roswell, and it left parts of itself everywhere.

I am sure that our army dudes gave it all back to the Greys. If our people were tricky enough to study all of that, they might have been able to make fast strides in science.

A spaceship that is tough enough to survive the trip from any star to our own solar system is virtually indestructible. There is no sane way that any force on Earth, whether it is the designs of man or forces of nature will be able to bring such a vessel down.

For such a vessel to make it here, it has already survived kinetic impacts that dwarf the power of our greatest nuclear weapons. It would float serenely from the midst of the worst that we could throw at it.

I get one of those headaches when I consider impossibilities. If Tiger Woods loses a game of golf against a ten-year-old girl that has never swung a golf club, I get one of those headaches.

When I am told that a species that is competent enough to come all of this way to visit us, but that species is also so incompetent that they crash their craft in places conveniently accessible to Native Earthlings, I get a migraine.

No, the only reason why alien craft occasionally crashes and are recovered by humans is that the aliens want the craft to be recovered by the locals. It is probably an attempt to upgrade our tech without admitting that they are attempting to do so.

Perhaps they do actually struggle to live with some Prime Directive that dictates that they cannot influence the locals by giving them technologies. Maybe this is just a shady way to have it 'fall off the back of the truck.'

By this time, I do not have to say that Occam's razor says that the aliens must be crashing their craft intentionally. It would be virtually impossible to bring an interstellar starship down. If you did bring one down, if the aliens did not want humans to get their sticky little hands on what was left, they could beat our time getting to the site to recover the craft. They could also confiscate the pieces anytime they wanted to take them.

No, the aliens are playing a long game that requires us to become more familiar with the alien technology. I am a little too pessimistic to believe that our visitors are trying to help us, but part of their plans appears to need us to advance our technology ASAP.

It could be that they are in some form of war where we qualify as troops. It could also be that they think that we will either prove to be controllable by them before we become a serious technological threat. We might also be destined to be assimilated into their species long before we become that threat.

They must be frustrated by the way our governments and corporations are attempting to keep all the cool new tech to themselves. They cannot control access to the technology forever. One day soon it must flood out into the public.

We need to advance in a lot of ways if we hope to survive the next couple of centuries. This technology could help with that, but we must ask ourselves if following the breadcrumbs is in our best interests in this particular case.

Time will tell if the path we are on is the right one. Regardless, asking us curious George talking monkeys to not try to find other people's secrets never works, so we might as well find out stuff.

15 FAMILY

The universe must contain aliens of every possible shape. It must contain aliens of every possible size. It has to contain aliens of every description. The only ones that we report here on Earth that we see are bipeds with two legs two arms and one head. Any Theory or hypothesis about human-like alien visitors must explain this discrepancy.

It is a convenient inconsistency when humans only see human-looking aliens. If you noticed on Star Trek (pick any series), you would notice that almost all of the aliens on the show are human-like or hominid as well. The few that are not hominoid usually use a proxy such as Mr. Spock or some human or humanoid in their activities to give them that human flavor.

The truth is that we only identify with other creatures that are similar to humans either human inform or personality or both. We love our pets, but it is because we enjoy watching them do things that seem similar to what we do that makes us enjoy them.

The fact is that we are somewhat limited in our ability to empathize with other creatures. We only really empathize with creatures in which we can see ourselves acting in their role. Unfortunately for human beings that usually means they have to be human to some extent. If they are not at least somewhat human-seeming, then we may find it way too hard to identify with them.

If you think this is incorrect, then imagine your favorite Star Wars movie but replace all your favorite characters with some alien starfish or octopus or worms, or maybe some of them can be snakes. You would probably not enjoy the movie that much, especially the Romantic parts. Our primary concern when it comes to an event is in its effect on our species or on ourselves. It is not a stretch to extrapolate that humanoid aliens would be attracted to investigating us, and non-humanoid ones would tend not to be that interested in us.

If aliens were also related to us as we suspect, would they not be that much more interested in us? I think that it is safe to believe that an alien bipedal humanoid would be interested in humans for the same reason that we are more interested in bipedal humanoid aliens. If they have a standing family invitation to Thanksgiving dinner, they might well have a vested interest in investigating us.

We have already advanced the theory that the reason the aliens contact us is because they are in some way related to us. This is a good time to think about how this could possibly be true.

One of the reasons why we should consider the aliens to be related to us in some manner is because of what I like to call biocompatibility. If an organism is in a new environment, it interacts with the other native organisms in that environment either by not reacting at all or by resulting in mortality either for the new organism or for the old ones.

Usually, the organisms on one side or the other finds itself to be infected by some sort of deadly plague from the other side. If the genetics are not similar, either the new or the old genetic life form could be subjected to a fast plague or no reaction whatsoever. Almost certainly, the new organism would have no ability to actually consume any of the other organisms and get any value from it.

When an organism finds itself in a new environment, there is a high mortality rate of that organism until it acclimates to the new environment. Foods are poisonous, bacteria are deadly, and every aspect of the environmental system kills the newcomer.

Eventually, the descendants of the organism change to adjust to the environment. The diseases become less lethal. Some of the foods become digestible, and they do not poison the organism. After a few generations, the descendants of the Life Form are at home in the environment.

This is how new species learn to tolerate their conditions. The foods we eat are good for us because we have adjusted to eating them. If an organism, such as an actual alien, were thrust into an Earthly environment without a heritage of acclimation, they would be dying like flies.

This suggests strongly that the aliens we see either have inherited some of the human traits that helped us survive the environment or they have existed here long enough for them to acclimate to the environment due to their own exposure to it. It is possible that the aliens are shielded from our planet's biosphere, and never actually come into contact with organisms of Earth. This does not seem to be consistent with the reports of their activities.

The aliens could have a history of living on Earth that is as long as our own history. This could be either present or past history inhabitation of the planet. It seems unlikely that they lived on our planet while we lived here, but it is not impossible. Do not forget that we have not successfully bagged a Bigfoot yet, and we know they live here if they live at all.

They could have inherited our acclimation to Earth's environment by sharing genetics with us. This probably means that they originated here, or they developed from the same genetic start as Earth life. It is not impossible that our alien visitors were seeded by another species with Earth compatible genetics.

This brings us to genetics. Our DNA is based on four of potentially thousands of different amino acids. As far as I understand it, our DNA could have been based on any four, or five, or six amino acids. This would make genetic material that is incompatible with our current genes.

The most likely ways that aliens could have compatible genes to ours is if their genetics was born in our waters, or in a parallel worldline that duplicates our timeline until after random choice picked the four amino acids to use building DNA.

We use the four amino acids in our genetics and another sixteen amino acids in some function of our bodies. That is a total of twenty amino acids out of over a hundred. The twenty amino acids our bodies use are Alanine, arginine, asparagine, aspartic acid, cysteine, glutamine, glutamic acid, glycine, histidine, isoleucine, leucine, lysine, methionine, phenylalanine, proline, serine, threonine, tryptophan, tyrosine, and valine.

Other amino acids are likely to poison our systems or pass through our system without being assimilated. The likelihood that a truly alien being could possess our *exact* amino acid heritage is tiny. They almost *have* to be our relatives.

16 EXPATS

The history of the genus Homo Sapiens is routinely extended after one discovery, or another insists that humans existed further back in time than formerly thought. Science currently admits that humans have existed a little more than 200,000 years. Do not be surprised if that number is revised to even older soon.

Consider the current belief that humanity has completed all of his technological advancements beyond the Clovis point within the last 10,000 years. While I do not agree with that assessment, it does bring up an interesting point.

There has been little or no change in the potential for humanity to innovate since the conservative origin date of 200,000 years. During the last ten thousand years, we have advanced from hunter-gatherers and primitive farmers to space capable. If we descended into a dark age tomorrow, it would be as a species that could have had space colonies.

If we have been around for two-hundred-thousand years, then humanity may have advanced to the level of space capable **twenty times** during that time. If our species has been around even longer than that, then we might have had even more chances of having planted space colonies during our history.

One of the ways that the so-called aliens could be compatible with us, but be as different appearing as they are is if they are Returnees. If humanity has a much longer history than is generally accepted by established science, the species could have risen to high technology and fallen into dark ages many times during that history.

Perhaps our species has traveled to the stars in one or more of these civilizations. Once there, it is likely that they would have to modify themselves to adjust to the many different environments that they encountered on the worlds they attempted to colonize.

That would certainly explain the genetic compatibility of the aliens, as well as the technology and variety of appearances they exhibit. If they do not come from parallel Earths that is the most probable answer to their history.

Another reason that they may be compatible and bipedal is that they may indeed share genetics with us, but for a different reason. They might be **Seeders**, seeding life like themselves across the universe.

They would almost certainly use compatible DNA in the seeded life forms. They would probably use their own genes to create a new life form, only changing it as much as needed to get the results they wanted.

Seeding is another possible way that the genetic compatibility could have occurred. Seeding could have also taken place from panspermia, the process of life spreading from planet to planet protected inside of rocks that become asteroids.

This material would be ejected into space by impacts and could carry starter genes through the universe. This would explain the possession of the same genetics, but it would *still* be very unlikely that the intelligent descendants of that Panspermia would be hominoid.

As you may have suspected by now, my favorite theory is that the aliens come to our Earth from parallel universes. This would quickly explain their genetic compatibility and their hominoid forms. It answers most of our questions.

The next thing that we shall discuss is the possibility that the aliens are presently residing on our fair planet. This is certainly not as unlikely as it sounds. Even without the high technology, there are many places where these beings might hang out without getting busted by us Normals.

After we explore the local people theory, then we will be looking at an origin in parallel universes. Beyond the normal origins such as these, we will also consider time travel as a possible source of our 'alien' visitors.

17 INTERNAL

This is the chapter where we will examine the possibility that the so-called aliens are not alien at all. They *could* dwell on or inside *this* planet, or even on the surface in a non-monitored place, or under the ocean. Perhaps they are original inhabitants of this world, or maybe they came to live here from another place in our universe a long time ago

It is most likely that they are original to this world because they would have to have been around long enough to precede the establishment of Earthly life to have compatible genomes to ours if they were not original. That would mean a history of billions of years on Earth.

There are huge sections of the ocean floor, and even of the Earth's surface that has never been explored in any comprehensive and systematic way. There is also an unknown number of subterranean caverns that could house billions of the hypothetical aliens.

The aliens could hide in the Amazon Rainforest for a

long time without worry of being found. There are many places in Antarctica and the Australian Outback where they could comfortably hide an alien city or two for as long as they might want to stay hidden. They are tight-lipped about it, but all the recent buzz about a new discovery on Antarctica makes me wonder.

For creatures with high technology, I would advocate that the most likely place that we could find whole cities of these aliens would be deep under the surface, in subterranean tunnels, or hiding perhaps at the bottom of the Marianas Trench or some other deep place.

There are two to four hundred cities submerged beneath the sea. They are at depths from one hundred to four hundred feet deep. Several unexplained massive structures have been detected, such as the Bimini Road, undersea 'crop circles' and the like. There is certainly plenty of room to hide an alien incursion in the ocean's depths.

There have been sightings of UFOs emerging from the waters all over the world. Many such reports are associated with places like the Bermuda Triangle, and other places related to weird events, but there are many reported in areas that have no such claim to fame.

Some people suggest that UFOs may emerge from underwater volcanic vents, emerging from the interior of the Earth, using the vent as an exit point. This seems a bit far-fetched, but it would be hard for me to refute the possibility. This leads us to the idea that if the aliens were actually terrestrial, they might be found *inside* of the Earth, deep under the surface.

There have been many reports suggesting that alien aircraft have been seen exiting from exits in the earth's crust. The Hopi Indians had several relevant legends about alien visitors. They spoke of Sky People, Star People and even of the Ant people. According to the Indians, the Ant people lived underground, and twice they saved the Hopi people from extinction, even allowing them to live with them underground for a short time. If I did not know any better, I would swear that the Ant People depicted looks suspiciously like a standard Grey.

Beyond the seas and the underground, there are plenty of places where alien types could hang out without being seen on the surface of the planet. I consider that it is possible, but I think that we are reaching a point where we should start noticing major settlements on the surface any day now.

The technological level of the aliens, either living under the ocean or underground, could be at almost any level, as long as they could procure proper nutrition, water, and air. I know nothing about the alien needs nutritionally, or their ability to deal with water and air problems. I can only speak to the needs of humans in those positions, so that is what I will do. I would expect aliens to have comparable, even if different, problems to human beings in those circumstances.

Assuming that humans get a sufficient level of proteins, fats, carbohydrates, vitamins and trace minerals in their diets, they would be okay below ground or beneath the sea. Humans do not produce their own vitamin C so they would have to obtain the vitamin from something that does produce the vitamin. For vitamin C, usually, people just eat citrus fruit or any of a number of other plants with high vitamin C content. Mushrooms are one of the few crops that will grow in the Earth's interior, which could provide Vitamin C, but nowhere near enough to supply a human's dietary needs.

Maybe our hypothetical Ant People Grey could go topside to raid the local orange grove at night. Maybe they do not need it. You decide. Another problem would be getting enough vitamin D, which you usually can get by sitting out in the sun for a few moments. If you are deep underground, that could be a problem for you.

If you are in an ocean colony, that would not be a problem. The Livers of most of the bigger ocean predators, such as the shark, are so rich with vitamin E and A that you could die from an overdose if you ate it. Such sources would offer an adequate supply of vitamin D. Not knowing what needs an alien might have, it is hard to decide what problems they might have, living in these environments.

Suffice it to say, fulfilling *all* of the needs of a common organism, which is not evolved to live underground or in a city beneath the sea, is another game of wackamo. Fulfill one of the needs, and find a hundred others you never thought of.

You may have noticed by now that I am not a proponent of the idea that the aliens come from this planet, and that they could be living beneath the sea, or deep underground. I would be willing to consider the idea that they have mastered the ability to disguise themselves, and are currently and quietly living amongst us.

I would be ready to discuss the possibility that aliens may have established underground and undersea bases, either by their lonesome or in conjunction with the military of the US or other countries, as some have suggested. They may have long-standing underground stations, and the Hopi might have been taken to live in one of these in the past.

I believe that they could live in those conditions for extended periods of time. I just doubt that they live there permanently.

18 PARALLEL

My favorite theory of what reported aliens are is that they are human analogs from alternate Earths in parallel universes. I have many reasons for believing that this is correct. There is nothing that requires that parallel worlds are the only origins, of course. Some of them may also be Expats from former human civilizations that are returning to Earth.

It would probably be good to supply a little background on what parallel worlds are, and what makes them a viable reality. I am going to paraphrase myself a little to explain parallel worlds and universes to you. I wrote a book called THE LAYMAN'S GUIDE TO QUANTUM REALITY in which I explained the subject in more detail than I can afford to devote here.

In the past century, some variations of an experiment called the Double-Slit experiment was carried out with puzzling results. This experiment involved placing a photographic plate behind a barrier with two slits cut into it. A single electron or photon was directed to the barrier, and the photographic plate was there to document which slit the electron went through.

In quantum mechanics, this is seen as a two-solution problem. The electron should go through either the left or the right slit. Whichever one it went through is considered to be the 'real' solution, while the other slit is considered to be the potential solution, which was supposed to be shown as unreal as soon as the real one was resolved.

If reality depends on the probability of a single electron going through one of the two slits, and the chances are 50:50 for it to go through either, then each path is equally likely. The problem that the experiment discovered is that when the experiment is unobserved, then the electron shows that it went through both slits in equal intensity by the interference pattern. Increase the number of slits, and you change the probability and intensity of the interference patterns for it to go through each slit.

When they brought in the Observer, they saw that the electron only went through one of the slits, as though it was a bullet. Unless you believed that the electron knew when it was under observation, you had to believe that the situation remained unchanged *from the Observer's viewpoint.*

Some physicists were never all that happy with the throwing away of potential solutions willy-nilly in quantum mechanics anyway. Everett, under the tutelage of Dr. Wheeler, looked for a way to explain the strange evidence of such experiments as the double slit experiment. The simplest explanation was the Many Worlds Theory. The

Many Worlds Theory was an add-on theory to Quantum Theory.

Everett needed a theory that explained the quasi-reality of all of the possible outcomes of an event, such as the interference pattern shown in the unobserved experiments, and the almost mystical effect that the Observer's presence had on the outcome that 'turned out' to be the real one.

The most straightforward explanation was that the 'unreal' outcomes really existed, even in the presence of the Observer, but from the viewpoint of 'our' universe, we could not see them anymore. Imagine the scenario from a slow-motion standpoint.

Imagine the Observer, who is as much a part of the Quantum Universe as the electron he or she is observing. Is it possible that the Observer is as much a part of the examined quantum system as the particle path? If so, and if the two possible paths of the electron are potentially real, then is it possible that there are two versions of the Observer watching the experiment that is also potentially real?

Let us assume that both outcomes are real. One version of the Observer sees the electron go through the left slit. The other Observer sees the electron go through the right slit. From the moment of the event, each of these Observers is in a separate worldline, where the result they observed is the real one, and the other possible outcome was the one that did not happen. These two worlds are right here, but a half-twist away and neither world is able to see the other one.

For the Many Worlds Theory to be valid, we must show that all solutions or outcomes of quantum events are real. For the solution to be 'resolved' in each universe, there should be an Observer that exists to see each of the solutions as the real one. Each solution forms a new worldline in which that solution is the real one. There is ultimately only one 'real' solution. The only initial change to each new worldline branch is the Observer and the outcome. The universe branches at each event.

The Origin Universe is arbitrary. Timeline history of new branches of the universal tree is the same for all new branches up to the branch point. With a nearly infinite number of events occurring in each universe each second, each one spawning a new set of universes, the tree of universes has an essentially infinite number of branches, themselves branching at an increasing, and essentially infinite rate. Parallel Universes are Cospatial. The separation between universes is caused by a separation of realities induced by quantum properties rather than by space-time separation.

There have been reports of humans and other things crossing the veil between these parallel worlds. It is possible that the human-form aliens that are reported come from one or more of these parallel universes.

Since they are related to each other, most of the details of existence will be the same in each universe. Parallel universes are related to each other. All of the events in two given parallel Earths will be the same, until that one fateful event that splits off one shadow world from another.

For us to encounter the inhabitants of one of these

universes that appears to come from a far-flung future, we just need to pick a proper worldline. Let us imagine two such parallel Earths interacting with each other to produce a long ancestral line in what looks like a shortened timeframe.

Let us call them World A and World B. World A follows our own timeline, with everything happening in it as it would in ours, but due to a long-past event, it advanced along the timeline at an accelerated rate, making it appear to be an Earth of the far future. World B is our universe.

Imagine that World A has advanced to a point where the form of humanity is essentially the Greys as described in contact reports. They have migrated out into their version of the universe and made a general nuisance of themselves. At some point, they decide that there are good and valid reasons to create a less advanced version of the species, to do some sort of tasks, or to act as watchdogs, or to fight a scary enemy. They might have done it for all kinds of reasons.

There exists a variety of presumed hybrids called the Nordics by the contactees. They are tall, white, and human-appearing. They may be what history called the Anunnaki.

If these alien-human hybrids are indeed the Anunnaki, then the Greys must have brought them to our universe up to 30 million years ago. Sometime after that, either the Anunnaki were left on their own, or, more likely, they revolted against their masters, and started their own empires.

These hybrids apparently established themselves on Mars

for a few million years, until someone evicted them using nuclear weapons. They eventually made their way back to the shadow of their own birth planet, about 430 thousand years ago. Everything after that is our possible history.

All of this is the purest speculation, of course. Too many of the variables are unknowns to apply Occam's razor. I tend to like the idea, because it does explain several aspects of the problem, including the universal human-form contacts, evident genetic advancements and the frequency of visitation, but it is still just speculation.

19 TIME

The only remaining source of the alien visitors that retains a certain level of plausibility is that they are time travelers from Earth's own far future. I do not personally ascribe a lot of confidence to this argument for some reasons that I will try to outline in this chapter.

There are a number of reasons why time travel is not a practical and useful process. Let me explain how time travelers find that they did not travel in time after all.

There are too many reasons why the Many Worlds interpretation of quantum mechanics is true to ignore it and its consequences. Let us apply our reasoning to a simple time travel mission.

The usual definition of a dimension is that it is an accessible pathway for movement. For instance, a coordinate plane is a two-dimensional object, with an x and an y dimension. You can move along the x or the y axis in either direction. You can go to $x=+20$, or you can go to $x=-20$. You can do the same with the y-direction.

In the ordinary world, you cannot move backward in time, so time does not really meet the definition of a dimension in this sense. It is more appropriately considered to be a property of the laws that govern mass and energy that allows the Observer to distinguish points within the process of event completion.

For instance, if the event is the burning of a piece of paper, a sense of time will allow you to distinguish each point during the event where the process is at each point between the beginning and the end of the event. You cannot go back to the beginning when you wish to do so, and you can only reach the end-point in the usual way, by living through the event to that point in the timeline.

Do not misunderstand me. Time travel is *possible*. It just is not practical, or useful. Allow me to educate you.

You can use a singularity, such as a wormhole, to move to any point on the timeline you wish to move. There is no place that a wormhole cannot access. It is just that after you get there, you will find that you never traveled in time after all.

Imagine that you built a wormhole manipulating time machine, and you went back in time to kill Uncle Hitler while he was a baby. You hopped into the machine and set the dials for April of 1889.

After a brief acclimatization, you found the future tyrant in his crib, and you strangled him to death. Just when you were about to return home to enjoy the fruits of your temporal labors, your time machine was stolen by a group of Irish Travelers and melted down to sell to the railroads.

Luckily, you had your immortality shot, so you decided that you would just wait for the 'present' to get here. What is a century or two of waiting to see the perfect world?

You spend a century or so tweaking the world just a bit, to make it that much more perfect. Finally, the moment you still look at as the 'Present' finally arrives. Guess what? It is nothing like the world you left.

The fact is that the second you appeared in your past, it was not your past anymore. There was one object in the universe that was not in the original timeline. That object was you.

When you changed the first event, you caused the timeline to branch at that point. While you certainly changed the world around you, that world was no longer in *your* history.

Keeping all of the previous in mind, the 'aliens' that we see could easily be the hominoid descendants of Humanity of the far future. They could be, but they would not be from *our* future.

It is unlikely that anyone using a singularity to visit a past point would be able to find their way back to their actual 'present.' It would be useless to them since any benefit they gleaned from their own world could never get back to that world. Only if the purpose of the visit was to live in a different timeline would the visit have any benefit to anyone.

No matter how the technology worked that brought them here, the introduction of the new events in our timeline, or their past timeline, would cause branching of parallel universes. When they arrived back in their own time, they would discover that all they had accomplished was to create a parallel branch of reality. The past of their timeline would remain unchanged.

The double slit experiment indicates that the Many Worlds Interpretation of quantum mechanics is valid. If this is true, then time travel is not practical for all of the reasons I have indicated.

Time travel is not practical because if you go back in time, you create a new worldline branch, and your original branch is unaffected. The person who goes back in time and changes events, intending to modify history, will see history change if they stay to watch. However, that history is not the original history, which is unaffected. In other words, you can time travel, but it will do you no good.

The ineffectiveness of time travel will prove beyond doubt that the Many Worlds Interpretation is correct, as it is required to produce paradox-free time travel. Stable wormholes will still be useful for instantaneous travel from point to point.

We hardly need to roll out the Occam's razor on this subject. The logic is simple. The Many Worlds Interpretation is true. All time paradoxes are negated by worldline branching at each event created by time travelers. Time travelers cannot travel into the past without creating a paradox. A worldline branching creates a new timeline, which all Observers and events introduced to the original past will occupy.

At the end of any travel to the past by a singularity, you

have a new branch of the timeline with new events, and the original timeline is unaffected. There is no way to get there from here!

20 ANALYSIS

Now is the time to start applying Occam's razor to the mass of factoids that we have discussed in the previous chapters. Once we have strained out all the unlikely conclusions, we can conclude this book by painting the scenario of what is most likely to be the correct answers to the question of alien life.

We introduced Drake's Equation in chapter 1. Plugging in the best numbers we have, we established that the galaxy should have thousands of worlds with life. We also decided that the galaxy should currently have hundreds of intelligent technological aliens with the ability to broadcast signs of their existence to us.

In chapter 2, we started looking at the flood of reports of alien activity. These reports have been submitted not just for years, or decades, but for centuries. We noted that there are some similarities between the old folktales of the Fairy Folk or Sidhe abducting or interacting with humans and the interactions and abductions reported by the modern aliens.

The sheer number of reports made suggest that some common events are responsible for the belief by so many people that they are interacting with aliens. While it is possible that the reality we live in is an unreal reality, it does not seem to have the sort of inconsistency that one would expect to be present from the different points of view present in a large mass of reports.

We acknowledged that we could be living in a consensus reality based on holographic or other informational technologies. If this is true, the information seems to be consistent enough to allow us to treat reality as though it were materially real. For our purposes, we agreed that we could assume ourselves to be living in a material universe and that the events, which include alien activities, should be assumed as what they appear to be, actual interactions with entities that appear to be aliens.

We noted that the caliber and volume of Observers make it hard to imagine that the reported alien activities are substantially different from the reports in chapter 3. At this point, we agreed that Occam's razor leads us to believe that aliens are real and that they are coming here to visit us.

We discuss in chapter four the technology required to get here from any interstellar location. We agreed that to make it here, the aliens would have to either be substantially different physically and psychologically from human, or be in possession of a warp drive, gravity control, effective shielding, and probably inertial control.

We decided that such a technology would not be vulnerable to anything that our planet has to offer. We must assume that anything that happens concerning these aliens is intentionally done by them.

In chapter 5, we examine the evidence left behind on Earth by all the aliens. They obviously cannot come and hang out with photographed entities. Apparently, they are forbidden to come out to Earthlings, unless one of the boats 'crashes', or some other calamity forces them to leave behind information or objects. They are bright enough to engineer some accidents to allow these interactions. Think of Captain Kirk just trying to get shore leave with one of those green women.

In the next chapter, I introduce what I like to call the Recursive Anthropic Principle. It is a complementary tool to use in logical arguments in concert with Occam's razor.

The Recursive Anthropic Principle is the idea that one should not attempt to prove a conclusion which is not beneficial to oneself. There are many aspects to a conclusion of an argument that is never stated, but that are important. Those who argue should argue for those conclusions that actually bring them what they want, in addition to what logically fulfills the needs the argument addresses.

Under the RAP, if one is arguing for purchasing a car, but secretly desiring a red Camero, then one should argue for the Camero that they actually want. It is a nod to the realization that acquiring the physical needs does not necessarily supply the emotional needs of a situation.

It is also true that some of the conclusions that one might reach that are the most logical are also the least useful to one. For instance, if one is a prisoner in a prison with a

100% mortality rate over time, and with no successful escapes in its history, the most logical conclusion is that you cannot escape this prison that will kill you. It is most logical, but it is a conclusion that will not aid you to survive. In fact, it will kill you, so you should not seek to prove that conclusion.

In chapter 7, I point out that modern science believes that humans set idly by for 190,000 years doing nothing. In the last ten thousand years, humans apparently modified all of their pets, cattle, and crop plants, conceptualized and built cities, learned to read and write, and essentially built civilization within a couple of thousand years.

Our alternative concept is that Humanity might have risen and fallen many times during the time he has existed. He might also have existed far longer than currently thought. We have also just found out that life has existed on Earth for over four billion years.

Chapter 8 was a basic recap. We note that the aliens appear Hominoid, yet alien. If a directive was in place to hide visitors as not alien, then they are doing a lousy job of it. It is obvious from the major activities that aliens are reported to be engaged in that they are primarily interested in human genetics.

You can tell from the way aliens apparently follow human bloodlines through the generations that they are interested in an ongoing process, and not simply the genetic material itself. If they were just cataloging genes, they could make a single visit for specimens, not multiple visits to the same contactees.

In chapter 9, we explore the mounting evidence that human civilization has been around a lot longer than modern science will admit. There are a large number of cities submerged offshore around the world in 150 to 400 feet of water, suggesting that the cities were built when the ice sheet held that much water out of circulation during the ice age. These cities appear to be between 11,000 and 29,000 years of age. There are a few settlements that seem to have been devoted to gold mining that may be over 100,000 years old.

We discussed the Sumerian Empire and the Anunnaki in chapter 10. We noted that the writings of the Sumerians did not have that flavor of fiction, but was more in the vein of journaling.

In chapter 11, we briefly discussed the Rama Empire, Aratta, Atlantis, and the creator gods that seem to share certain traits. We implied that history cuts deeper into the past than traditionally suspected, and with higher technology.

We discussed the possible places that the 'aliens' are actually from. We noted that they could be local, interplanetary, interstellar or from a parallel universe. We decide that they are probably not from the interplanetary system.

In chapter 13, we discuss the peculiar aspects of human genetics, genetics on Earth versus possible genetic makeup on other planets that would have developed independently of Earth, and the various aspects of the human form that tells us things about how we got those characteristics.

Given the level of technology and durability of the craft that would be necessary for any ship to make it to Earth, in chapter 14 we examine the likelihood that crashes, and other unlikely mistakes could take place by accident. We are left with the disquieting feeling that the only reason why we can glean some small materials from alien craft is that they want us to have it to examine.

In chapter 15 we put forward the assumption that the aliens we see are actually related to humans in some way. This is the reason why they bother to come to see us in the first place and explains some of their goals when dealing with us.

In chapter 16 we examine the way in which the aliens are related to us in a little more detail. We examine the possibility that they are returnees from past human space colonies that have returned to Earth after centuries of self-directed genetic modification in the natural course of adapting themselves to various environments.

In chapter 17 we briefly examine the possibility that the aliens are a related off-shoot of humanity, but they never left the planet. It is possible that they have lived below the surface, under the ocean, or even in out of the way places on Earth all of this time.

In chapter 18 we covered the possibility that the aliens were human variants from a parallel universe, related to us because they are what humans have become in an alternate worldline. We had to distill a basic coverage of the Many Worlds Interpretation of quantum theory down to a few pages, and then explained how it would relate to seeing aliens, so it was probably the most confusing part of this little book.

In chapter 19, we finally got around to discussing the possibility that the aliens we were seeing were actually not aliens at all. Instead, they could be humans from far distant future times who have perfected time travel and used it to travel back to visit us.

I am rather proud of how quickly we caught and skinned that snake before it could get into the henhouse to steal all of our intellectual eggs. We showed that time travel is possible, but it winds up not being time travel after all.

There are some concepts that one has to nip in the bud. Never let a teenage boy master the concept of invisibility. Don't dirty up the time stream with time travel. That is how you deal with things like that.

In conclusion, we will be laying out our findings throughout this book, applying Occam's razor for the final time, and trying to sort out the most likely conclusions from the evidence. It should be a hoot!

CONCLUSION

We are finally at the conclusion of the book. Just like the conclusion of the argument, we will be putting each sub-conclusion in its place and trying to make a sensible explanation for what the alien activity is all about. Along the way, we will be utilizing Occam's razor to pick the most sensible conclusions.

Numbers don't lie. Chapter 1 and Occam's razor told us things we needed to know about life, the universe, and Everything. The answer wasn't 42, because Drake's Equation dealt us a bigger number than that for the number of presently existing intelligent aliens alive and well in the galaxy today.

We combined the numerical likelihood of intelligent alien existence in chapter 1 with the reports of alien visitors in chapter 2. Noting that it is best to assume that what we observe is real, and not dementia, we decide that Occam's razor tells us that we are actually being visited by aliens who present themselves as hominoids. We also note that writings from ancient civilizations tell us that these visitations and activities have been going on for thousands of years.

We decided that the simple answer to why the aliens look and act the same over the entire world, no matter how credible the Observers are, or what experiences they have had in the past, is because what the Observers are seeing is substantially what is happening.

We decide that the technology needed to get here from any interstellar position is invulnerable to any force we could bring against it. Whatever happens to the aliens is exactly what the aliens want.

We get the distinct impression that the alien visitors are under some sort of regulations that tells them not to advertise their presence. This means that any interactions that successfully tells humans that there are any aliens around have to look like an accident. It is obvious that the aliens are going out of their way to have accidents in all sorts of out of the way places.

In chapter six, we discussed a property of logical argument that I like to call the Recursive Anthropic Principle. It is intended to be a companion tool to Occam's razor.

We admitted that logical arguments do not necessarily have logical, or even rational, conclusions. Some conclusions cover the admitted requirements for a conclusion, such as four wheels and an engine for transportation.

Other unstated requirements are just as important. It

may be absolutely necessary emotionally for the car that you are seeking to be a sports car. If this is so, you need to be arguing for obtaining that sports car.

The point of the Recursive Anthropic Principle is that the argument is being conducted for your benefit, so any conclusion that you argue for should be one which is beneficial to you as well. Just as the Anthropic Principle says that only in a universe which allows life is there life to ask why is the universe so pro-life, the RAP says that an argument is a tool used by the organism to get it what it wants. It should never forget that the tool it uses is for its own benefit, and the direction it seeks to travel should also always be to its benefit.

We point out in chapter 7 that science proposes that modern man set twiddling his thumbs for most of the time since he evolved living as cave dwellers. For unknown reasons, modern man apparently developed architectural knowledge, subsidiary technical skills, and the ability to develop modern crops and cattle from the wild versions, conceived of and developed laws, reading and writing, and the various business and trading skills it takes to survive a civilization.

They insist that we did this despite all the problems. Human knowledge builds on previous existence. We learn how to build cities by building cities. The first ones will probably be disasters. If we are going to change a non-nutritious wild grain into a domestic crop plant, it will take hundreds of generations of plants, all raised by people with the knowledge that nobody will be able to eat the grain for many years.

It will take about as long to develop domestic sheep, hogs, and cows as to breed the crop plants. For several generations of the animals, the potential herdsmen must securely fence the animals or lose them. They have to feed them and devote attention to them. They have to put more energy into holding them than they will get from them as food, eggs, help, or milk.

Modern discoveries suggest that human evolution might have given humans much more than 200,000 years in modern form, although nobody knows how long. During the two-hundred-thousand years, our species still had time to have developed a high civilization and possible space travel several times over.

Between the very real possibility of 'space gods' giving humans a 'leg up' technologically and a lot of time to advance, it is nearly inconceivable for humans not to have had prior advanced civilizations. Occam's razor would say that the idea of space level technology for humanity in the past is a near certainty.

In chapter 8, we noted that the aliens that are seen are hominoids, with a walking gait that is derivative of a human gait. This suggests that either they are more closely related to humans than are the local primates, or we are forced to push the concept of parallel evolution to ridiculous lengths.

Consider the depth of the alien interest in human genetics, and the interesting idea that they are hominoid in appearance but not mistakable for a human, and it would appear by Occam's razor that the aliens are related to us, interested in us as closely related to them, and actually look like what they appear to be to us. The likelihood that a non-hominoid species could disguise themselves as a hominoid species, but could not complete the disguise to appear human is preposterous.

In chapter 9, we discussed the evidence that human civilization has been around much longer than modern science admits. We talked about the many cities around the world submerged below 150 feet of water, and estimated to be older than 9000 years old.

We also discussed the odd factoids, such as a human footprint inside a fossilized dinosaur footprint dating back millions of years. While I do not personally think that is because humans existed way back then, it may be evidence for the sort of useless time travel discussed in chapter 19.

Sometimes you can tell if someone is spinning a story, or if they are simply repeating history, as they understand it. The Sumerian's records about the activity of the Anunnaki sounds like they are talking about real history, not about stories that someone made up.

We noted in chapter 11 that the stories of the gods seem to share certain similarities worldwide. If you couple that with all of the major indications of worldwide interactions with places that were not supposed to know about each other, and it certainly looks as if there was a continent-spanning civilization in the deep past that connected all of the old empires.

We noted the many indications of very real places such as the Rama Empire, Aratta, and Atlantis. We began to suspect that history cuts deeper into the past than traditionally suspected, and with higher technology.

We discussed the possible origin places of the 'aliens.' We noted that they could be local, interplanetary, interstellar or from a parallel universe. We decided that they are probably not from the interplanetary system.

In chapter 13, we discuss the peculiar aspects of human genetics that might be of interest to the 'aliens.' Genetics on Earth would necessarily be of a different genetic makeup than on other planets that would have developed independently of Earth.

Knowing the level of technology and durability of the craft that would be necessary for any ship to make it to Earth, in chapter 14 we recognize how unlikely it is that crashes, and other mistakes could take place by accident. We begin to have the disquieting feeling that the only reason why we can glean some small materials from alien craft is that they want us to have it to examine.

It has become plain to us that the aliens we see are actually related to humans in some way. This is the reason why they bother to come to see us in the first place and explains some of their goals when dealing with us.

When we examine the way in which the aliens are related to us in a little more detail, a myriad of connections come to light. We examine the possibility that they are returnees from past human space colonies that have returned to Earth after centuries of self-directed genetic modification in the natural course of adapting themselves to various environments.

We briefly examined the possibility that the aliens are a related offshoot of humanity. This would be like an Expat group that went into space, but they never left the planet. It is possible that they have lived below the surface, under the ocean, or even in out of the way places on Earth all of this time.

In chapter 18, we covered the possibility that the aliens were human variants from a parallel universe, related to us because they are what humans have become in an alternate worldline. Without re-explaining the Many Worlds Interpretation of quantum theory here, it would explain a lot of the questions related to seeing aliens. I like the idea, but I know that many of you will find the whole concept a little bit mind-numbing.

In chapter 19 we finally got around to discussing the possibility that the aliens we were seeing were actually not aliens at all. Instead, they could be humans from far distant future times who have perfected time travel and used it to travel back to visit us.

It is time to wrap this small book up by rehashing the events related to aliens using Occam's razor to establish what is likely the correct conclusions. I will try to narrate those events as a history of aliens and alien visitation. I hope that it will work for you.

About 4.55 billion years ago, the Earth was formed and existed as a hellish, molten planet. The universe was nearly ten billion years old at that point. It is reasonable that alien life already existed many places in the universe by that time.

It has recently been discovered that life was present on this planet barely 200 million years later. If that was the beginning, life began as a form of extremophile one-cellular organism in what was still hellish conditions, but it was here.

We do not know if it actually originated here, or if it was brought to our planet embedded in asteroids in the process known as Panspermia. It could even have been brought here by a beneficent alien species.

I personally tend to believe that life arose here naturally. I see no reason to believe that life is so complicated that a world with millions of unique little spots to act as cradles to new life would have a problem bringing it forth. Bringing aliens into the process adds unnecessary cooks to the meal, and Panspermia still requires that Life had to have arisen *somewhere.*

Life developed from simple Prokaryotic cells to the more complex Eukaryotic cells, and then it made the jump to multi-cellular forms somewhere between 700 million and 500 million years ago in the ocean. There was no life on the land until about 450 million years ago when primitive fungi provided the vital service of terraforming the soil so that green plants could thrive there.

The subject of human interactions with aliens usually advances the proposition that humans might not originate on Earth at all. Unfortunately, the genetics forming during this initial phase of life on Earth disagrees with that proposition.

In order for an alien to bring an alien life form to Earth that is enveloped seamlessly into the genetic tree of the planet, the alien would have had to tinker with the budding life during this budding phase, from 4.3 billion to 430 million years ago. It is possible, but I really do not consider it realistic.

According to Occam's razor, the human genetic line *did* originate here on this planet, and it really *is* related to the other primates and more distantly to every other species on this planet. It is just as obvious that *something* has tinkered with the genetics of our species.

Our genetic material has all the genes of the primates, but it contains 243 unique genes of unknown origin. Our #2 and #3 chromosomes have been glued together, giving us a total of 23 pairs of chromosomes, while our primate cousins all have 24.

Many of our modifications make little sense, unless they exist because the tinkerer took a coffee break, and forgot to come back to finish the job. For instance, when we got superior mental faculties, we lost the massive strength that our primate relatives all have. Anyone in the field can tell you that the loss of such an important trait does not occur because of a mutation for another survival trait.

Our leg and foot components really suck for efficient travel. We have the endurance and toughness of an overprotected hamster. We are overly subject to Diabetes, cancer, heart issues, and genetic disorders of all types.

If we were products of natural selection, and no genetic manipulation had occurred to make us what we are, we would not have so much junk DNA. Occam's razor pretty well insists that genetic manipulation was involved in both our development and the development of our crop plants and our cattle.

Between the appearance of our visitors and the rest of the arguments for the hominoid appearances, Occam's razor is confident that the visitor's we report are all related to us. While it is possible that they have been hiding in or on the Earth, or on one of the other planets in the Solar System, it is most probable that they are either from another star or from a Parallel Earth. We discounted time travelers most effectively.

The most likely scenario for them coming from the nearby stars is that they were part of an earlier Diaspora. They might have left Earth a couple of hundred thousand years ago, modified their own genetics for survival into several different forms, and are now considering either returning to Earth or reconnecting with us in another sense.

Whichever reason they are interested, they have been busy with genetic tests. They might be attempting to find a hybrid form, correct a deficiency in their own form, or one in ours.

I reluctantly think that the Expat theory of who the aliens are is probably the correct one, given all those centuries where modern science suggested that humans sat around and did nothing. I have little doubt that humanity has been spacefarers at least once before this, and probably several times.

While I think that Occam's razor favors the Expat theory, I really love the Parallel World theory, and I hope that it is found to be the true origin of the aliens sometime in the future.

I hope that you have enjoyed this book, and I look forward to you reading the next book in the series shortly. Look for it at your favorite retailer soon!

The End

ABOUT THE AUTHOR

JD Lovil writes both nonfiction and fiction books. He is the writer of several How-To and speculative nonfiction books, as well as several cross-genre science fiction novels, dealing with the existence of a multitude of parallel earths as required by the Many Worlds interpretation of Quantum Theory. Originally from Arkansas, JD Lovil now lives in Phoenix, Arizona.

∞∞∞∞∞∞∞∞

Most of my books are available in paperback, and some of them are available in audiobook formats, in addition to the digital format.

If you enjoyed this book, please consider leaving a positive and honest review where you bought your copy.

Other books published by me can be seen at

www.jdlovilbooks.com

You may connect with the Author on:

Facebook at www.facebook.com/jd.lovil.9

Pinterest at www.pinterest.com/jdlovil9

email at jdlovilpublishing@gmail.com

Consider reading book two in the Occam's razor Series

Coming Soon!

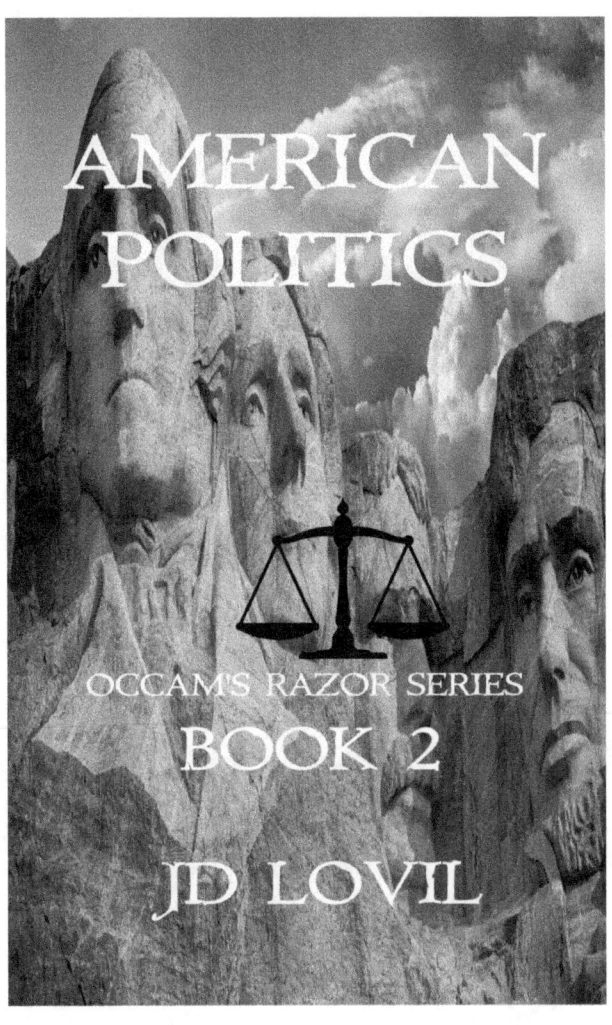

If you enjoyed the book you just read, you might also enjoy

THE LAYMAN'S GUIDE TO QUANTUM REALITY

Here is an excerpt of that book for you:

Chapter Three of
The Layman's Guide to Quantum Reality

3 LAWS OF QUANTUM THEORY

The way I see it, Quantum Theory started as a mathematical exercise in probability calculations, and ended up being an exercise in metaphysics. Quantum equations yield general solutions. A general solution is a 'plug and play' solution. A general solution is a solution, which yields specific solutions when you substitute specific variable values into the general equation. In many cases, one valid solution set of a general solution is the positive and negative number values of 'the answer.'

Because there are more than one specific solutions to quantum equations, it is necessary to calculate a probability of finding the system with which the equation is concerned in one state, versus finding the system in a different state. This simple calculation of probabilities became complicated when Heisenberg came up with his Uncertainty Principle.

Heisenberg stated that certain data must be forbidden to know by the Observer of an event. He was talking about events in the microscopic world of elementary particles, such as electrons. His simple claim that the Observer can know one part of the status of a particle, but knowing that information will exclude the Observer from knowing a piece of complementary information or data about the particle's status at the same time blew a lot of Physicists' minds.

You can know the momentum or location of a particle, but not both at the same time. This was intended to apply to the microscopic level only, and Heisenberg never intended it to apply to the macro-scale universe. Particles are neither particles nor waves but are 'smeared' over the small space most likely to contain them, and this throws some of the variables of calculation into doubt at any particular measurement time.

You can measure the momentum of a particle by observing the effects via the use of your measurement device, or you can detect the particle position using your devices, but measuring either status increases the uncertainty of the other one because the measurement you can make is a probabilistic one rather than a certain and specific one.

Heisenberg was showing that specific solutions could not be made for all aspects of a probability equation because doing so would be to turn a general equation solution of probability into a specific solution with no probability uncertainty. Let us see the form for momentum (p) and velocity (v) of a particle.

The simple equation is

$$\Delta x \Delta p \geq h/4\pi$$

Remember that this equation calculates the uncertainties in x and p in relation to each other:

Δx is the uncertainty in position x

Δp is the uncertainty in momentum p

$h/4\pi$ is a constant number. For our purposes let us call it C and say that it is equal to 1. As a probability calculation, remember that the uncertainty in x or p cannot be zero, nor can the number usefully be incalculable.

$\Delta x \Delta p \geq h/4\pi$ becomes $\Delta x \Delta p \geq C$ becomes $\Delta x \Delta p \geq 1$

$$\Delta x \geq 1/\Delta p \text{ and } \Delta p \geq 1/\Delta x$$

When the uncertainty in position x falls to certainty because it has been measured, by definition and mathematics, the certainty in the momentum p must decrease, and vice versa. We do not have to solve the equation to see that this is true since each of the uncertainties in this equation is in the reciprocal form of each other.

Physicists promptly jumped on the idea of this being a demonstration of 'The Observer Effect.' The Observer effect is the idea that you cannot observe a particle without bumping it with some force used in the measurement, making it different from what the measurement shows after the measurement. While this is generally true in the process, it has nothing to do with Heisenberg's Uncertainty Principle.

A couple of different Observer-related relationships were revealed in the aftermath of deriving the Uncertainty Principle. The first was the effect of observation itself, where the Observer defined the property of the particle by observation and found that he was affecting the uncertainty of the complementary properties by changing the probability mathematics that the observation yielded. The second was the Observer Effect mentioned in the last paragraph, where the act of observation perturbed the system being observed, changing the status of the particle after observation of part of the system of properties.

One of the traditional experiments that demonstrated the effect of an Observer on a quantum system was called the Double Slit Experiment. It has been done in various formats since 1801, and it involved sending a photon or electron toward a plate with two thin slits cut into it, through which the particle can pass, and a photographic plate behind the plate to record which slit the particle came through.

It was noted that the particle would apparently pass through both slits and cause an interference pattern on the photographic plate if nobody was watching the experiment, indicating that it had passed through in its waveform, but it would pass through a single slit as a particle if somebody were watching the experiment. The acuity of observation was important to the results as well. If a high detail camera were placed strategically to watch the experiment, the experiment would show particle properties. Turn the camera off, and the experiment would show wave properties.

A physicist named Schrödinger was irritated by the metaphysical turn that quantum theory was taking, and so he proposed a joke thought experiment that has become known as Schrödinger's cat. This is how it went.

Schrödinger told the tale about a cat, enclosed in a box, with a device that was guaranteed to release a poison and kill the cat exactly 50% of the times that the lid to the box was sealed. The cat had a 50:50 chance of being dead in the box, and the same chance of still being alive.

With tongue in cheek, Schrödinger asserted that the cat was neither alive nor dead until the Observer opened the box and looked inside. At that time, he would see that the cat was alive, or that the cat was dead, and his act of observing that would make it so. He wanted to demonstrate that the metaphysical viewpoint of that situation was ridiculous and that when the Observer opened the box, all that was happening was that he was now able to see which result was the real one. To Schrödinger, it was a simple probability problem, and it had nothing to do with some arcane power that the Observer generated.

The strange thing about Quantum Theory is that Schrödinger was right, and wrong at the same time. The cat in the box was a simple fifty percent probability calculation. The presence or absence of the Observer probably would have had no effect on the outcome of the experiment. Probably.

The double slit experiment indicates that the Observer *is*

an integral component of the outcome. In the case of the double slit experiment, the outcome appears to be different when the Observer is present. The Observer resolves which solution is real.

We should note here that quantum events are not usually considered on the Macro level because what we see in our world is a swarm of trillions of particles. Each one of these particles is engaged in quantum activities, but in the quantities that are required for us to notice them, the outcomes of the aggregate events statistically smear out into an aggregate statistical approximation of Standard or Newtonian physics.

We will get deeper into the nature of the Observer's interaction with the reality around him or her in a future chapter. For now, let us paint a stranger picture of the quantum world. Only after we discover the true nature of reality can we explore what effect we might have on that reality.

We have touched on the fact that particles of all sorts have both a wave-like and a particle-like nature. The fact is that everything shares in this wavicle nature, but for macro-objects, the statistical smearing causes the wavicle nature to pass unnoticed.

In what I will call Traditional Quantum Theory, all 'particles' have both a wave and a particle form. Since all of the Macro Objects we see around us are composed of these particles, they too have this 'wavicle' form. The reason we do not see the waveform of the matter around us is due to the statistical nature of large numbers of particles. Just as large numbers of charged objects tend to cancel charges, so too does a large number of waveforms tend to cancel each other.

In Standard Quantum Theory, all transitions of energy levels, and therefore of the position are instantaneous and nonlocal. There are minimums of distance and duration which are indivisible. This is because everything, including space and time, is quantized. No duration of time exists less than

$$10^{-43} \text{ s}$$

There is no distance or length that exists that is less than

$$1.6 * 10^{-23} \text{ m}$$

These are the Planck distance and duration constants. Think of time and distance are composed of bricks of these sizes, instead of little points with no volume. Since there is no distance less than $1.6 * 10^{-23}$ m, if a particle is moving, it must of necessity instantaneously jump or teleport at least these tiny distances in the process. Only if space is composed of a substance with no minimum distance can Newtonian movement work without some form of discontinuous 'teleportation.' Otherwise, teleportation must be a part of the movement process.

These events are not restricted to be local events. They have smaller but still valid chances of being nonlocal. These transitions of distance are valid for any distance larger than the Planck minimum. It is not forbidden for an electron to transit to extra-galactic positions, although the chances in any one case are vanishingly small.

Let me give you an example of a nonlocal event. As we know, Einstein claimed that there was no speed greater than the speed of light. If we wish to act or transmit information, you cannot do so at any speed greater than the speed of light. Quantum Theory disputes this by the concept of entangled particles. We will get back to what that means in a moment.

Assume that we are flying across empty space in the good ship Lollipop when some unknown god decides to materialize a star about a light year away. Einstein said that our ship would not feel the gravity from that ship for a year, at the same time that we could see the star existed by the light that had just traveled to us.

Quantum Theory says not so fast. We have changed the information that is part of the quantum equation for the system, and this information may be able to travel at any speed. If an electron can travel galactic distances instantaneously in a small percentage of electron transitions, you may also feel the effect of a new gravitational well a light year away instantaneously.

If it takes a year to feel the effects of the new gravitational source, that is an example of a local process. If it is felt instantaneously, or less than a year later, it is a nonlocal process.

Quantum entanglement is a nonlocal process. If two

electrons interact with each other, it has been shown from a series of experiments that the properties that each display may be affected by what is done to the other one, no matter where they are in relation to each other. If you flip the spin on one of the electrons, the spin on the other one may also flip, no matter how far away the second electron is away from the first one.

The subject of nonlocal events and entanglement will come up in many guises in the chapters of this book, but now we return to a primary component of Quantum Theory. Quantum states are calculated for any considered system using the Schrödinger equation. I will not be going through the Schrödinger equation here, as it is a little more complicated than I suspect that most of my Readers want to get in mathematical explanations of the theory.

The solution to the Schrödinger equation is a general solution. This means that the solution of the equation is another equation that will yield the specific solutions that apply if you have specific parameters, or that will yield the set of all specific solutions. For instance, if you have a general solution of

x=n where n is defined as the set of all integers

...-3,-2,-1.0, 1, 2, 3...

Then specific solutions can include x=-3 or x=0 or x=2 and so on.

The point is that quantum equations have more than one

solution. Standard quantum theory says that only one of these solutions turns out to be the True solution, and the rest of them are just potential answers that turn out not to be the correct one. Going back to the double slit experiment, this meant that the electron had a 50:50 chance of going through either of the slits in the plate.

The fact that the unobserved experiment indicated that the electron went through *both* slits suggested to the Experimenters that the equation was *unresolved.* This meant that if the experiment was unobserved, the correct solution was not made real. It was only if somebody observed the experiment that one of the two possibilities showed itself to be real.

In Standard Theory, this meant that the Observer's presence was necessary to resolve which of the solutions was real, and collapse all of the other forms of the equation, making only one of the solutions real. The rest of the solutions were unreal.

Seen one way, this just meant that the Observer was a part of the system necessary to collapse an equation solution set into one true one and other false ones. Seen another way, the Observer occupies a metaphysical position of power in the creation of our reality.

In the great year of my birth, Hugh Everett proposed a theory that came to be known as The Many Worlds Theory. This theory said that all solutions to a quantum equation were true. When the Observer resolved a particular solution as true, he resolved it for just his universe. The decision point of each event was a place that the universe would branch into a new worldline for each of the possible solutions for that event.

This meant that if the Observer saw that the electron went through the left slit of the two slits, that was true for the universe in which the Observer continued to experience. However, the Observer would also see that it had passed through the right slit in another universe, which had split off from the common worldline at the instant of the event.

I am not going into any more detail on the Many World Theory at this point since I will be covering the subject extensively in the next few chapters, and aspects of the theory in several subsequent chapters. Put on your protective helmets. It is going to be a wild ride!

Also by JD Lovil

EBOOKS
Fiction

WORLDSHIP PRAXIS

SHADOW OF WORLDS

VANGUARD OF MAN

JIGSAW WORLD

THE HAND IN SHADOW

Non-Fiction

THE LAYMAN'S GUIDE TO QUANTUM REALITY

LOSE WEIGHT NATURALLY

WHACKING HAPPINESS

THE WRITER'S PLAN

UNKNOWN VISITORS

HITTING YOUR GOALS

PAPERBACK

Fiction

WORLDSHIP PRAXIS

SHADOW OF WORLDS

VANGUARD OF MAN

JIGSAW WORLD

THE HAND IN SHADOW

Non-Fiction

THE LAYMAN'S GUIDE TO QUANTUM REALITY

LOSE WEIGHT NATURALLY

WHACKING HAPPINESS

THE WRITER'S PLAN

UNKNOWN VISITORS

HITTING YOUR GOALS

AUDIOBOOKS

Fiction

WORLDSHIP PRAXIS

SHADOW OF WORLDS
VANGUARD OF MAN
JIGSAW WORLD
THE HAND IN SHADOW

Non-Fiction

THE LAYMAN'S GUIDE TO QUANTUM REALITY
WHACKING HAPPINESS
UNKNOWN VISITORS
HITTING YOUR GOALS

If you enjoyed this book, please consider leaving a positive and honest review where you bought your copy.